PENGUIN V

THE LONE WOLF

Neha Dwivedi, a Kargil war martyr's daughter, is a doctor by profession and writer by passion. She is an alumna of Delhi Public School, R.K. Puram, and Lady Hardinge Medical College, Delhi. She sought solace and found her strength in writing post her father's martyrdom.

She now lives in Delhi, where she works as a childbirth educator and an infant and young child feeding specialist. She deeply believes in the healing and inspirational power of stories. Her first book was *Vijyant at Kargil: The Biography of a War Hero*.

THE UNTOLD STORY OF THE RESCUE OF SHEIKH HASINA

THE LONE WOLF

Foreword by

MAJ. GEN. IAN CARDOZO,

author of *1971: Stories of Grit and Glory from the Indo–Pak War*

NEHA DWIVEDI

PENGUIN
VEER
An imprint of Penguin Random House

PENGUIN VEER

USA | Canada | UK | Ireland | Australia
New Zealand | India | South Africa | China

Penguin Veer is part of the Penguin Random House group of companies whose addresses can be found at global.penguinrandomhouse.com

Published by Penguin Random House India Pvt. Ltd
4th Floor, Capital Tower 1, MG Road,
Gurugram 122 002, Haryana, India

First published in Penguin Veer by Penguin Random House India 2021

10 9 8 7 6 5 4 3 2

This book is a work of non-fiction. The views and opinions expressed in the book are those of the author only and do not reflect or represent the views and opinions held by any other person. This book is based on a variety of sources including published materials and research, conducted by the author, and on interviews and interactions of the author with the persons mentioned in the manuscript. It reflects the author's own understanding and conception of such materials and/or can be verified by research. All persons within the book are actual individuals and the names and characteristics of some individuals have been changed to respect their privacy. The objective of this book is not to hurt any sentiments or be biased in favour of or against any particular person, political party, region, caste, society, gender, creed, nation or religion.

ISBN 9780143452720

Typeset in Bembo Std and Minion Pro by Manipal Technologies Limited, Manipal
Printed at Thomson Press India Ltd, New Delhi

www.penguin.co.in

Contents

Foreword

I feel grateful to Dr Neha Dwivedi for bringing the life of Colonel Ashok Tara, VrC, to centre stage. This is the man who rescued Sheikh Hasina and the family of Sheikh Mujibur Rahman from certain death at the hands of the Pakistan Army during the Indo-Pak war of 1971.

Every citizen of India and Bangladesh needs to know about the stellar part this brave officer played. His act of supreme courage and strong mental focus not only saved the lives of the family members of 'Bangabandhu' Sheikh Mujibur Rahman, but also cemented the relationship between India and Bangladesh, and took it to new heights.

The book highlights the issues of 'fear' and 'courage', which are two sides of the same coin. Courage is the antithesis of fear, and Ashok Tara, through his attitude and behaviour, proved that fear originates in the mind and it is there that it needs to be destroyed. The book highlights how at the age of nine, Ashok Tara, while walking through a forested area, came face to face with a snarling wolf. Inspired and motivated by his grandfather, a shikari, he stood his ground and made the wolf back off.

This experience, at a young age, stood him in good stead many years later, during the 1971 war, when he came face to face with a group of trigger-happy Pakistani soldiers, holed up in a house along with the family of Sheikh Mujibur Rahman. A few moments earlier, these soldiers had killed an unarmed correspondent, who had approached the house seeking a story, in cold blood. They were not aware that all Pakistani forces in East Pakistan had surrendered and they could, if pushed, have assassinated the entire family of the Sheikh and also Ashok Tara who approached the house unarmed.

It was an extremely tense moment and the situation could have swung either way. Much depended on the attitude and conduct of Ashok Tara, who was a major at that time. The Indian officer, with his resilience, and physical and moral courage, however, managed to mollify the Pakistani soldiers. What eventually happened is history and is narrated vividly by Neha in this spine-chilling book.

The moniker *The Lone Wolf* given to Ashok Tara by the author is very apt. This story of cold courage needs to be known, understood and remembered by the world at large.

20 October 2021
New Delhi

Maj. Gen. Ian Cardozo,
author of *1971: Stories of Grit and Glory from the Indo–Pak War*

1

Staring Down a Lone Wolf

The seemingly normal walk back from school through the forest suddenly took a dangerous turn as young, nine-year-old Ashok found himself staring directly into the eyes of a wolf that was no more than thirty yards away. Not surprisingly, the sight stopped him in his tracks.

In the year 1951, much like the rest of the country, Delhi was still coming to terms with its fledgling independence. Unlike the urban behemoth it is today, back then the capital was mostly made up of open land and agricultural fields interspersed with extended swathes of wilderness. It took less than a decade for the city to begin shedding its agrarian roots. The vast openness gradually gave way to the demands of a functional city: residential areas, intertwined with commercial establishments. But in 1951, four years after Independence, Delhi was still in touch with a certain wilderness.

It was in this year that Ashok Tara's family left their serene and spacious residence in Baird Place for East Patel Nagar, a relatively busier part of Delhi. The DAV school that used to be at a convenient distance of one kilometre from Ashok's Baird Place residence, was now all of 10 kilometres away. But his new neighbourhood gave him the opportunity to indulge in his favourite activities, like exploring the neighbourhood and hunting down pigeons with his slingshot. He especially enjoyed taking part in the events organized by the society committee during festivals, like the rath yatra: a procession of a tableau borne on horse-drawn chariots in which he would play Lakshman and sit alongside another boy playing Ram from the Ramayana (one of the two Sanskrit epics of ancient India).

Despite the promise of adventure, the long distance he had to travel to get to school and back not only involved greater travel time, it also posed a certain amount of danger. Ashok and Kirti Tara, his elder brother, now had to pass through Rajendra Nagar, a semi-occupied colony and a forested ridge behind Birla Mandir (Gole Market). The only transport available to them was a single-route, Delhi Transport Corporation (DTC) bus that set off at 6 a.m. and returned only before sunset.

The brothers had to catch this bus, even though classes began at 8 a.m. and ended at 1 p.m. The route of the bus was circuitous: West Patel Nagar Depot–East Patel

Nagar–Willingdon Hospital (now Ram Manohar Lohia)–Gurudwara Bangla Sahib, where the brothers disembarked and the bus continued onward.

Willingdon Hospital, founded by the British in the year 1932 for their own government staff, was situated adjacent to the Gol Dak Khana of today and came under the jurisdiction of the New Delhi municipal committee post-Independence. A few years later, in 1954, it was transferred into the purview of the central government, but retained the same name until the 1970s, when it was changed to Ram Manohar Lohia Hospital, after Dr Ram Manohar Lohia, a socialist, political leader and a popular activist in the Indian Independence movement.

Like clockwork every morning, at about 6.10 a.m., Ashok and Kirti would catch the same bus along with other early commuters—most of them still sleepy. But the Tara brothers would be wide awake and always sit in the front seats of the bus, eager to take in the view through the windscreen and enjoy the cool morning breeze before alighting at Gurudwara Bangla Sahib.

After a hasty Partition, Delhi particularly experienced a mass influx of Punjabi refugees from West Pakistan, who had chosen to make India their home. The Bangla Sahib Gurudwara, located at Connaught Place in the heart of Delhi, with its notable golden dome and tall flagpole known as 'Nishan Sahib' would be buzzing with activity at any given point of the day. Worshippers would arrive in groups to offer prayers, meditate or just perform *seva* (service) by way of paying their respects to their guru. Today, this structure is much more magnificent, complete with large marble entrances and additions of other architectural extravagances. Even in those days, with its tranquil *sarovar* (a holy lake situated inside the complex), it served as a haven for anyone who sought peace and solace. There was a garden outside with date and jamun trees where children and adults alike spent their time plucking fruits.

After a bone-rattling journey aboard the rickety and dusty DTC bus, Ashok and Kirti would proceed straight to the gurudwara to offer prayers and get *prasad* (sanctified food), halwa and puri, which had been cooked by the people doing seva. This had become their breakfast. They would finish their breakfast, rinse their greasy hands in the sarovar and proceed to school.

Ashok's school was about one kilometre away from the gurudwara, while Kirti's, a separate branch of the same school, was closer to the gurudwara. With time weighing heavy on their hands before their respective classes started, the brothers invariably took a detour through the gurudwara's orchard and filled their pockets with dates and jamuns, some of which they ate themselves and the rest they saved for distribution among their classmates and the children of the school peon. Thus, more often than not, even before school started, both the brothers would have purple-tinged pockets on their crisp white uniforms to match their purple-tinged teeth.

*

Born to Chattarpati and Damyanti Tara, Ashok belonged to a fairly large family with two older brothers and one younger sister. Ashok and his siblings grew up with stories of World War II as their father had donned the military uniform during the war. Their learning didn't end with just the stories of the war; they were also reared on a strong set of values and encouraged to believe in what they knew, learned or heard rather than on any unfounded and irrational fears or superstitions.

The Tara children were intrepid and always on the lookout for adventure, unlike most children of their age, who tended to be more timid. On their way to school from their house at Baird Place, the Tara brothers took a shortcut through a graveyard. While most other children either avoided this route or passed hurriedly through it, Ashok and Kirti would stroll leisurely past the gravestones and, on their way home, would even tarry a while to play marbles in the quietness of the cemetery. As most people in their neighbourhood were steeped in superstition, Ashok and Kirti would often come across earthen pots containing fruits or coins being burned with herbs in the middle of the pathways, to supposedly ward off the evil spirits. Whenever the brothers espied these simmering pots, they would waste no time in kicking them aside, quickly picking the fruit and pocketing the coins, before ambling away nonchalantly.

The extended journey to school from their new home was more of an adventure rather than an inconvenience for the two brothers, one that they couldn't wait to embark upon every day.

However, Ashok was still a little boy, barely nine years old. His adventures were always under the watchful eye of his elder brother. Kirti, as a senior in school, had to stay back for certain extra-curricular activities on some days. Whenever Kirti couldn't leave at the same time as Ashok, the plucky nine-year-old had to make the trip back home alone.

The route included a kilometre-long walk through Birla Mandir and then across the thickly forested ridge that added another kilometre or so to the Taras' daily trek. The boys had to cover all of that on foot before they could reach the main road to hitch-hike which, in those days, meant thumbing a ride on a bicycle, flagging down a bullock-cart or a push-cart, or hitching a ride on an odd bus. They had quickly realized that, in the relentless Delhi summers, after a long and tiring day at school, their trek home felt more like penance than an adventure. It was an understatement to say that trudging through the dusty forest paths, with the trickling perspiration making their shirts stick to their bodies, was exhausting.

The ridge, which is a northern extension of the ancient Aravalli Range, some 1·5 billion years old, extends from the southeast at Tughlaqabad, branching out in places and tapering off in the north near Wazirabad on the west bank of the Yamuna river, covering about 35 kilometres. It is also known as the 'green lungs' of the city of Delhi. In those days, the undergrowth was wilder and more unspoiled than it is now. Furthermore, it wasn't merely called a forest, it was complete with dense foliage and dangerous wildlife as well. Today, as expected, there exists an urbanized version of it, with tourist spots like Buddha Jayanti Park, with ancient monuments nestled within it.

The forest ranger would regale them with hair-raising stories about wild animals—bears, wolves, monkeys, foxes and a variety of reptiles that roamed at large in this area. Every once in a while, he would go so far as to even lend them his stout wooden stick, which had an iron spike mounted on it (like a spear), for protection, especially from reptiles.

Ashok's class IV final exams were approaching when, just as in the recent past, Kirti told him he had a football match that was going to keep him from accompanying his younger brother back home. And so it was that a tired, but carefree, Ashok had to walk through the woods alone.

Just like every day, Ashok walked into the forest, exhausted and thirsty, but still alert, placing one foot in front of the other, hoping he wouldn't come across one of the reptiles that the forest ranger had warned them about. He was thankful for the light, albeit dusty, breeze that caressed his face every now and then. However, the eerie rustling of leaves made him look around to make sure he didn't have an unwanted companion. He wondered why, today of all days, he hadn't insisted on borrowing the watchman's stick because that would have definitely made him feel much safer. Ashok picked up his pace, hoping to traverse through the woodland as quickly as possible. The sooner he got out of the jungle, the sooner would he be able to hitch a ride home.

Ashok had barely gathered speed, when he froze in his tracks. With a loud crash, out leapt a massive wolf from the undergrowth and stood snarling in the middle of Ashok's path.

As the wolf and the boy faced each other, the ticking seconds stretched into what felt like an eternity as the lad realized just how vulnerable his position was. His legs felt leaden and that warm summer breeze that had felt balmy only moments ago now felt icy, like an invisible hand on the nape of his neck.

As if on cue, Ashok thought of his maternal grandfather, a keen hunter, fondly addressed as 'shikari' by the people of his village. The old man had often recounted his experiences to his grandchildren who crowded around, listening with rapt attention; and, in his storytelling sessions, he had shared much sound advice with his young audience. Ashok's grandfather had told the children:

> . . . when confronted by an opponent, even if it's a wild animal, stare at your opponent with a confident and stern expression. This show of courage will effectively deter them from launching an attack.

Ashok had never imagined that he would ever be in a position to apply that piece of advice, but he now took a deep breath, stood his ground determinedly and glared at the wolf.

Sure enough, after a few minutes, the wolf baulked, retreated and slunk back towards the bushes. Before Ashok could heave a sigh of relief, the animal halted and looked back. Ashok held his stance, his expression fearless and undaunted. The wolf slowly moved away, perhaps losing its will to attack, just as his grandfather had said. After the wolf had vanished, Ashok immediately changed his route and pelted towards the main road, his mind still reeling with what he had just survived.

As soon as he was on the road, he met two forest rangers and told them about what had just transpired in the forest. They said that they were aware of the wild animals in the forest and were actually surprised that he had made it out alive.

Upon reaching home, he excitedly narrated the chilling episode to his family. They could barely believe that such a young boy had stared down a wolf like a seasoned hunter and had lived to tell the tale. They assumed he was making it all up.

However, as days went by, they heard about similar sightings from the forest officers and realized that Ashok had been telling the truth.

When Ashok's eldest brother asked him why he had not thrown a stone at the creature or run away, Ashok coolly reminded him of their grandfather's advice of never provoking the opponent, especially if it were a wild animal. Even the slightest provocation would have resulted in an attack, was little Ashok's reply.

They say lone wolves are the most dangerous kind. Ashok had not only faced one by himself, he had also walked away from it unscathed and with a kind of empowerment that would stay with him for the rest of his life. His own father had often told his children how 'fear is nothing but a state of mind'. After that day, Ashok learned that it wasn't a meaningless platitude.

Little did he know that this chance encounter had perhaps taught him to turn into a lone wolf himself in the face of adversity and was going to carry him through the most dangerous moments of his life in much the same way.

That the significance of that event would be monumental to not just his life but to the history of the world, was another matter.

2

The East Pakistan Conundrum

November 1970

The Taras were originally from Rawalpindi in Pakistan, but Ashok was born in the historic city of Aurangabad in Maharashtra. The year was 1942, pre-Independence India, and Ashok's father was serving in the Burma campaign. From a young age, Ashok was enthusiastic about listening to his father's stories of his gruelling stint in the army. His curiosity earned him the moniker *fauji beta* from his mother, a harbinger of what destiny had in store for him.

By the end of the year 1970, a commissioned officer in the Indian Army for all of eight years, Ashok was the company commander of Alpha (A) company of the 32nd Battalion Brigade of the Guards, a counter-insurgency unit in southwest Mizoram and headquartered at Lungleh.

The battalion was required to watch over four villages—Haurang, Lungleh, Bunghmum and Dimagiri—located on the Lungleh–Dimagiri road opposite the east of the Chittagong Hill Tracts.

Ashok's company was deployed at Dimagiri, the forward post that shared its border with East Pakistan. The Karnaphuli river was the only thing separating Ashok and his company from the Pakistani post on the opposite bank. Ashok's task was to neutralize any cross-border movements of Mizo and Naga insurgents.

Being at Lungleh helped familiarize him with the local terrain and its culture. In order to successfully operate against insurgents, the army had to develop a cordial relationship with the locals.

Ashok joined the unit in the first week of December in 1970. On the eve of 23 December 1970, he visited a local teacher's house to wish him for Christmas. Such practices are considered the norm in these areas, especially to gain goodwill and to maintain contact with prominent people. The teacher was not at home. Instead, he met his grownup daughter, with two unknown young boys. Ashok could sense that the boys were uncomfortable in his presence and could not hold a coherent conversation with him.

In the middle of the conversation, one of the boys abruptly left the room. The purpose of Ashok's visit was to glean information about any insurgent activity in the town, keeping in mind that the locals were preparing for the Christmas celebrations. The two youths' suspicious behaviour put Ashok on high alert. Although he was unescorted during this visit, in order to avoid precipitating a crisis, he mendaciously told the teacher's daughter that he wanted to have a word with his armed jawans who were purportedly waiting outside. He quickly returned to the battalion and informed his commanding officer, Lt Col G. Clifton.

A special patrol was immediately dispatched but, by this time, the two boys had left the house. Later, it came to light that the youths were Mizo insurgents and had left in a hurry because they feared that Ashok had discovered their true identities. They had come into town to collect medicines and to celebrate Christmas.

During January 1971, Ashok moved to Dimagiri Post, to the west of Lungleh and southwest of the Mizo Hills, located opposite the Chittagong Hills, East Pakistan.

During this time, across the border, the then East Pakistan was on its way to witnessing what can only be described as the most catastrophic time that the country had ever seen since Partition.

Despite being the most densely populated province and the hub of one of the most lucrative resources (jute) of the country, East Pakistan had long been surviving under dismal conditions. The economic windfall from the jute trade was being directed towards the development of West Pakistan. It would reportedly only receive 25 per cent of the import money while making 70 per cent of it. This stunted the development of the province and resulted in appalling living and working conditions for the people.

Economic negligence aside, East Pakistan had the largest population of all the provinces, but all the political decisions about its welfare and development were being made by people who neither lived in the region, nor, as it appeared, were interested in understanding the needs of the people who did live there.

In addition to that, there was the longstanding issue of the state's official regional language that had made for much of the disenchantment in the hearts of the people of East Pakistan. In 1948, despite the concerted efforts of the people of East Pakistan to include Bengali, besides Urdu, as an official regional language, as it was spoken by the majority of the population, Mohammad Ali Jinnah clearly stated in his speech in Dhaka that there could only be one official language in the country. This short-sighted decision was viewed as an intentional slight against the people of East Pakistan.

One of the most stentorian voices that kept growing louder since the start of the harangue about the language issue was that of young Sheikh Mujibur Rahman.

Sheikh Mujibur, popularly known as Mujib, was born in 1920 and was politically active as early as 1940 as a member of the All-India Muslim Students Federation (AIMSF).

Upon opting for Pakistan during Partition, he moved to East Pakistan and studied law at the University of Dhaka. It was there that he founded the East Pakistan Muslim Students' League.

Mujib remained politically relevant and active in the years following Partition, speaking out against West Pakistan's violation of the rights of the people of East Pakistan. Over the years he also led several protests and activities that resulted in multiple arrests. In fact, in early January 1950, when Liaquat Ali Khan, then prime minister of Pakistan, arrived in Dhaka, Mujib led the Awami Muslim League in an anti-famine procession. He was imprisoned for two years at the time.

Finally, following the death of his predecessor, Suhrawardy, in 1963, Mujib came to head the Awami League that had gone on to become one of the largest political parties of Pakistan. The word 'Muslim' was replaced by the word '*awami*' that translates to common people. This was done in order to acknowledge and include all the other communities in East Pakistan.

In the following years, the unrest arising due to the continued neglect and disregard of the needs and the demands of the more populous part of the country, East Pakistan, kept growing. Even though the East Pakistanis were more in number, they were poorly represented in Pakistan's civil services, the police and the military. The Punjabis of the West despised the Bengalis of the East and considered them weaker than their own 'martial race'. The Bengalis' appreciation of the fine arts was ridiculed too.

According to some accounts, some West Pakistani officials, who were posted in the East, would often travel with their entire retinue of staff, down to their very own gardeners. That was the level to which they underestimated the capabilities of even the menial labourers in East Pakistan and belittled the experience and knowledge of the local people; it resulted in reducing the much needed employment opportunities for the East Pakistanis. The unfair discrimination by the West Pakistanis was blatant and complete.

Then came the Indo-Pak war of 1965. Although it was fought on the western front, the eastern side was left exposed and vulnerable by very little, to no, deployment of Pakistani forces. They felt abandoned, uncared for.

Understandably, during the time following the war, the feeling of being suppressed, disregarded and neglected continued to fester in the hearts of the citizens of what was by now popularly known as East Bengal, with no effort (by way of actions) being made to alleviate their sense of ill-usage by the ruling regime. East Bengal's strong desire for autonomy resulted in uprisings by the people and political groups alike.

Eventually, in the year 1966, a 'charter of freedom of the Bengali nation' was put forward by Sheikh Mujibur Rahman in the form of a six-point demand, which came to be known as the 'six-point movement'.

Point 1: The Constitution should provide for a Federation of Pakistan, in its true sense, on the basis of the Lahore Resolution, and a parliamentary form of government with the supremacy of legislature which would be directly elected on the basis of universal adult franchise.

Point 2: The federal government shall deal with only two subjects, viz: Defence and Foreign Affairs, and all other subjects shall vest in the federating states.

Point 3: Either of the two following measures (should be adopted) with regard to currency:

a. two separate, but freely convertible, currencies for the two wings may be introduced, or
b. one generic currency for the whole country may be maintained. In this case, effective Constitutional provisions are to be made to stem the leakage of capital from East to West Pakistan. A separate banking reserve is to be made, and separate fiscal and monetary policy be adopted for East Pakistan.

Point 4: Power of taxation and revenue collection shall vest in the federating units and the federal centre shall have no such power. The federation shall have a share in the state taxes for meeting their required expenditure.

The consolidated federal fund shall come out of a levy of a certain percentage of all state taxes.

Point 5:

(1) There shall be two separate accounts for the foreign exchange earnings of the two wings;

(2) the earnings of East Pakistan shall be under the control of the East Pakistan government, and that of West Pakistan, under the control of the West Pakistan government;

(3) the foreign exchange requirement of the federal government shall be met by the two wings either equally or in a ratio to be fixed;

(4) indigenous products shall move free of duty between the two wings;

(5) the Constitution shall empower the unit governments to establish trade and commercial relations and set up trade missions in, and enter into, agreements with foreign countries.

Point 6: A militia or paramilitary force shall be set up for East Pakistan.

This movement received intense support from the Bengalis of East Pakistan. The other side (West Pakistan), quite predictably, considered the movement as radical and a ploy by Mujib to incite separatism in the country.

As a result, the proposal was summarily rejected each and every time it was put forward.

Mujib was fast emerging as the most important political figure of the country and he had the trust and support of his people. If one side perceived him as a troublemaker, resulting in his repeated arrests and suppression, the other would come forward, united in their support by way of widespread protests, demanding his release and asserting the need for recognition and conservation of their ethnicity and culture. His popularity grew to such an extent that the people dubbed him '*Bangabandhu* (friend of Bengal)'.

However, the troubles of the East Bengalis were far from over. On 11 November 1970, a devastating tropical cyclone, Bhola, ravaged East Pakistan. The evening of the following day, around the same time as the local high tide, the cyclone made landfall on the East Pakistan coastline. Although the Pakistan Meteorological Department did radio a distress signal on the same day, '*moha bipod shanket* (great danger signal)', in the coastal regions, it meant little to the locals as high tides and storms were part and parcel of their already difficult lives.

Their ignorance cost the poor people of the region dearly. The cyclone was unlike any storm they had ever experienced. In addition to massive loss of life along the coastal regions, estimated to be between 3,00,000 to 5,00,000, although the unofficial numbers were probably higher, the magnitude of human suffering among the survivors made it one of the worst calamities in modern history.

At the time, it was specifically reported that, in the thirteen islands near Chittagong, there were zero survivors. The reconnaissance airplanes that flew low over the islands to take stock of the situation reported that the destruction was complete throughout the southern half of Bhola Island. Over 3·6 million people were directly affected by the cyclone with 85 per cent of homes in the area completely destroyed or severely damaged. The areas near the coast bore the maximum brunt of nature's fury.

The stories to come out of the suffering of the so-called survivors were chilling. One of them was about Choudhary Kamal of Manpura island (one of the unfortunate islands that had been in the path of the cyclone), written by Howard Whitten and published in the *Guardian* on 18 November 1970. He quoted Mr Kamal:

> We have buried 10,000, but as you see there are many, many left to bury. Everything has its limit. We have no proper food, no water to drink, nothing. Our rice is bad so we dare not boil it. We burn it and then eat it. That way it will not do us harm. One man has a cigarette lighter. While it lasts we can still burn the rice.

Another one of them, eighteen-year-old Madan Mohan Shaha, told Howard:

> I was clinging to a bamboo pole but a wave swept me out to sea. After six hours, at daybreak, it washed me up 15 miles away. I am the only survivor of my family. Another youth, Ziaul Huo, was carried from the populated area of the island and dumped four hours later so far away, that he returned only yesterday.

The ones who had survived by clinging to the trees showed Howard how the flesh on their chests and stomachs had been rubbed raw. When Howard told Choudhary that the governor of East Pakistan, Vice-Admiral S. Absan, was to set up emergency headquarters on the island, he was bitter for his people about the delay. He said:

> Not even a watchman from outside came here. Many planes flew over, but until yours, nobody landed. Make them help. Make them send food, pure water and medicines.

That a citizen of one country had to plead with a citizen of another to urge their own government to send them help to be able to survive was heartbreakingly tragic. The fact that Mr Kamal, Madan and Ziaul were just three of the hundreds of thousands was agonizing.

Many stories like these were published during this time. An article that came out towards the end of the year, on 30 December 1970, written by the very famous

New York Times reporter Sydney H. Schanberg was boldly titled 'After Pakistani Storm: Grief, Indifference' and threw more light on the plight of those who had survived. He described how

> An extended tour of the stricken islands and interviews with officials, survivors and relief workers disclosed tales of terror and heartbreak, madness and grief—and a chronicle of public indifference and delay in helping the two million miserable survivors.

His article gave accounts of various survivors that were heart-rending to say the least. He wrote about a man named Munshi and his family, including his wife and five children. How his wife, on seeing the first surge, began to cry, pleading,

> Save my children! Save me! Take me somewhere safe!

But there was nowhere safe. The family lost each of the children, one after the other, despite the desperate efforts of their eldest son trying to hold on to his younger siblings before being washed away himself. In the end, only the couple survived, witnesses to the sheer tragedy engulfing them; a situation which was only going to get harder and harder as they got used to the cycle of sleeping, waking and weeping, again and again. Being surrounded by so much death and devastation, Munshi thought:

> This must be doomsday.

Schanberg went on to describe the utter indifference with which the rest of the country was dealing with the calamity. An important excerpt of the article reads:

> The morning newspapers reported that the damage has not been as severe as that of the previous storm. Radio and television continued the usual programs. By nightfall, the official death toll was 50.
>
> In Islamabad, the national capital, in West Pakistan, a thousand miles across Indian territory, the size of the disaster was not appreciated by the government either.
>
> Though newspapers had begun to talk of tens of thousands of dead by Saturday (12 November 1970 was Friday) and by Sunday of hundreds of thousands, the Government figure did not rise above 40,000 until eight days after the storm—thereby confusing foreign governments about the disaster's magnitude and delaying international relief.
>
> Gen. Agha Mohammad Yahya Khan, the head of the military government, was on an official visit to Communist China when the storm struck. He returned,

> as scheduled, two days later, stopping in Dacca to make a brief aerial tour of the devastated area.
>
> 'I am very much distressed' he said afterward, adding that he had ordered all Government agencies to mobilize for relief.
>
> He then flew back to Islamabad—a departure that was to be criticized later by political leaders as indicative of the callousness of the Punjabi-dominated national Government in West Pakistan towards the Bengalis of East Pakistan. The eastern province has been exploited economically by the West since independence in 1947.

Any relief work that came the survivors' way was done by foreigners. However, even that was delayed due to Pakistani indecision, sluggishness and mismanagement. As a result, whatever form of relief came, was still delayed by ten harrowing days for the people who were suffering. To add insult to injury, the article revealed how even when India offered helicopters, transport planes, river craft and mobile hospitals, Pakistan turned them down. In fact, reportedly at a party in Dhaka a week after the storm when an air force pilot mentioned that he was under strain because of long hours of flying, it turned out that it was not because of any air-dropping relief work, but because he had been practising bombing and strafing runs. He explained:

> This disaster has made us terribly vulnerable. The Indians could walk right in and take over. We've got to stay alert.

Even in the face of one of nature's most terrible manifestations, the government and its defence forces were busy preparing for an unforeseen, man-made, apparently impending emergency. Mostly because 'their' people were not affected by it.

Thus, unsurprisingly, upon meeting and getting to know that he was a reporter, the survivors would angrily ask Schanberg to

> Let the world know what our Government did.

Schanberg also stated that three weeks after the storm, a key official told a foreign expert that no rehabilitation programme had been planned for the outer islands because they had not been included in the 1961 census. It was also said that because natural disasters were so common and so difficult to control in East Pakistan and because resources were so limited, the central government, pleading helplessness, had tended to ignore the disasters and invest its resources elsewhere.

However, this time, the envelope had been pushed too far. The utter and blatant neglect and disregard of the victims of the Bhola cyclone was the final nail in the coffin.

Thus, it was no surprise that, when the Pakistani general elections were held on 7 December 1970, the Awami League under Bangabandhu's leadership enjoyed a landslide victory. Having the advantage of numbers on its side, the party won a massive majority in the provincial legislature. Barring just two, they had won all of East Pakistan's quota of seats in the National Assembly. They had formed a clear and unmatchable majority.

On the other side, the largest and most successful party, called the Pakistan People's Party (PPP), was headed by Zulfikar Ali Bhutto. Bhutto was principally opposed to the idea of Mujib forming the government and his demand for greater autonomy of East Pakistan. Bhutto was also supported in his opposition by other political parties and the Pakistan military alike.

Although Bhutto later did try and talk Mujib into forming a coalition government with him as the president and Mujib serving as his prime minister, his first knee-jerk reaction was threatening to boycott the assembly. The assembly was scheduled to be declared open on 3 March 1971. However, due to Bhutto's pressure and the resulting deadlock, the then president Gen. Yahya Khan postponed it indefinitely. For the Bengalis this was nothing short of electoral theft.

However, the last straw was the voidance of the elections that were held and voted for in large numbers, by even the women of Pakistan (a practice which was uncommon). It was as if their president had not only ignored their informed and just decision, he had in fact dismissed it out of hand, terming it as the 'gravest political crisis'.

This time, the people of East Bengal were not only hurt, they were furious. Their last shred of hope, the dream of forming a government with one of their own, had been unceremoniously snatched away.

So much had been endured and justice had been denied. Left with no other choice, they rose in rebellion . . .

3

Adolescence in Delhi

Ashok and his siblings spent their school years in the heart of Delhi, as the winds of change swept through the city. In this state of constant flux, the brothers continued to be enthralled by their father's stories of World War II. Tara senior had been at the Burma Front, assigned to regular patrolling duty with the British Indian Army Pioneer Corps.

Of all the wartime stories, Ashok loved to hear the one where his father and other soldiers were surrounded by Japanese troops. While the Japanese withheld their fire, the Indian troops (mostly Sikh soldiers) fired warning shots and demonstrated their determination to fight back.

Whenever Ashok and his siblings were lucky enough to find their father enjoying his evening cup of tea when they came home, they would eagerly gather around him in their courtyard—an area open to the sky in the middle of their rambling three-bedroomed house. They would take turns to give him an account of their day and then beg for their favourite war stories. The sun would quietly sink into the horizon as Tara senior held forth and his admiring audience grew wide-eyed with wonder, curiosity and pride. Their father would sometimes repeat his stories; nonetheless the children were spellbound every time. They loved these true stories of action and valour and were very proud of their father, who had played his part in the war.

These narratives left an indelible mark on the personalities of the Tara children. They never hesitated to stand up for what was right. The need to protect and value the hard-won freedom brought about by people like their father and those who had sacrificed their lives for the cause was deeply ingrained in them. The young Taras grew up to be courageous and honourable.

One chilly winter evening, thirteen-year-old Ashok and his brother, Kirti, were returning home after playing a game of football with their friends. Both brothers leisurely strolled home, chatting about their exploits on the playing field. The boys didn't mind the nip in the air and were just as oblivious to the dust being churned up by passing vehicles. A commotion up ahead caught their attention. A man pelted down the road towards them with a small crowd in hot pursuit, shouting, 'Thief! Thief!'

Ashok and Kirti exchanged glances. The man being chased was probably a chain-snatcher or a pickpocket.

Words were unnecessary; they knew exactly what had to be done.

As the man drew close, the brothers quickly linked arms to form a barrier and when the thief skidded to a halt in front of them, the young boys kicked him hard in the shins. Taken by surprise, the man went sprawling in the dirt. Ashok and Kirti quickly held him down so he couldn't pick himself up and waited until the pursuers arrived at the scene.

The felon stopped struggling as soon as he saw a policeman approaching. The witnesses told the police about the brothers' quick thinking and heroism that had saved the day. Ashok and Kirti were given a rupee each for their presence of mind and quick action.

★★★

By the year 1959, Ashok had grown to be a tall, athletic and outgoing young man, with a pleasant personality and was all set to start college. Ever since he was a little boy, Ashok had harboured dreams of following in his father's footsteps and serving the nation by joining the army. However, that dream would have to wait. Ashok was an ace sportsman and he was looking forward to representing the football and cricket teams of Delhi University.

The Sanatan Dharma College had just been affiliated to Delhi University and Ashok enrolled in the bachelor of commerce course. This new college was at Anand Parbat, a picturesque location on top of a hill, surrounded by a rugged landscape and far from the hustle and bustle of the city. It was an idyllic setting for a college. The main building was a modified and well-maintained army barracks, adjacent to Ramjas School, Number 2 (North Delhi). In fact, in the early days, the office of the college was inside the Ramjas School complex until classes began in August 1959.

By 1960, the foundation stone for the permanent building was laid at Dhaula Kuan by the then home minister, the late G.B. Pant. The name of the college was changed to Atma Ram Sanatan Dharma College, as it is known till date. It was and remains, a co-educational college.

The new college was far from the city and not yet well-known. This meant that the first batch of students was small, which ended up being a blessing in disguise. Each class had fewer students per professor allowing for the establishment of a better rapport between the teacher and the pupils. The first batch of students had the privilege of studying under the guidance of a faculty eager to make a good impression on the students. Teachers like Mr Yudhishter, Mr Prem Nath, Mr Rudra Dutt, Mr Kumud and Mr Grover, along with the principal, Dr Rai, made a lasting impression on Ashok.

***

Ashok belonged to a family of strong and fearless personalities. It was not just his father and forefathers who were known for their courage and valour, the women of the family had also demonstrated exceptional strength of character in times of need. Ashok had grown up listening to their stories and imbibing these values.

There was a time when a poor family in their village sought his grandmother's assistance to help provide shelter and treatment for an ailing pregnant woman. The only available doctor happened to be in the neighbouring village and the only other woman in the family was too scared to undertake the journey because of all the horror stories she had heard about the dangers of venturing into the wilderness late in the night. The menfolk in the family were diffident about their ability to take care of a pregnant woman. So, Ashok's grandmother, who was neither superstitious nor timid, stepped up for the job. She had once packed her stuff into a clay pot and forded the Tavi river all by herself to visit her sick son. She assured the family that she was perfectly capable of accompanying the pregnant lady. True to her word, she quickly draped a shawl around her shoulders and then gently supported the expectant mother through their arduous journey to the adjacent village. She made sure that the mother-to-be was comfortable and maintained a non-stop flow of small talk to allay any fears arising as they traversed the eerie night-time jungle and the wide fields. They managed to get to the doctor in time.

If his grandmother's stories provided lessons on grit and determination, his own mother's narratives taught him the importance of one's duty. A teacher by profession, she taught for twenty-five years, in the Lahore Montessori School in East Patel Nagar. One day, she was getting ready for school when she learnt that her elder son had met with an accident. His condition was serious and he had been taken to Willingdon Hospital. She rushed to see him and after ensuring that he was out of danger, she went to school. When asked how she could leave her sick son in the hospital and go to work, she clearly stated that her students, who were also like her children, had their final exams on that day. Her duty towards them and her profession was no less binding than her duty as a mother.

His grandfather, the shikari, was also an immense influence in his life. When Ashok was about ten or twelve years old, his grandfather would sometimes take him along on his hunting trips. He had often explained to the lad that he never fired at a bird or an animal which was sitting still, catching them unawares. In fact, when he espied a promising target, he would ask Ashok to throw a stone in its direction to make it take flight.

Later in life, his grandfather was unfortunately struck by a partial paralysis, which hampered his movements. A proud man, he didn't want to be dependent on anyone and insisted on doing as much of his personal work as he could by himself and continued going on his brisk evening walks. One day, his family saw him return from his evening walk on a cycle rickshaw. The rickshaw-man told them that the old gentleman had walked too far and being too tired to walk back, had decided to take a rickshaw ride back home.

He had, however, been too proud to accept the rickshawman's help to climb into the vehicle.

The whole family had one thing in common: they did not operate according to the norms of society but carved their own path instead; they chose to stand by what they felt was right; and whenever given a chance, they served and protected the people who needed help. There was no space for any myths and superstitions in their lives. Ashok, as a result, had been steeped in the same virtues and was inherently protective of the people around him.

In college one day, during Mr Prem Nath's English lecture, two unruly students kept disturbing the class. Mr Nath ordered them to quieten down or leave the class. The enraged hooligans became more aggressive and resorted to hurling insults at their teacher. When the lecturer reprimanded them, to the horror of everyone in the classroom, they brandished knives at the hapless professor. The air in the room grew tense.

Unable to watch the humiliation of his beloved teacher, Ashok took matters in his own hands. Along with his friend, Vinay Dar, he swiftly proceeded to disarm the rogue students before evicting them from the classroom. With the rest of the class ranged against them, the young thugs were clearly outnumbered and they left the room. Mr Nath heaved a sigh of relief and thanked Ashok for his timely intervention.

The months following this saw Ashok's esteem rise in the hearts of the faculty members and students alike. So much so that, when the university elections came around, even though politics was the least of Ashok's interests, his friends coerced him to stand for the post of supreme councillor. Thanks to the support of his classmates who had campaigned enthusiastically for him, he won the contest by a large margin.

By the end of college life, what Ashok lacked in academics he more than made up for in the field of sports, as he had always dreamt of doing. He proved his mettle by successfully captaining both the football and cricket teams to victory in their respective tournaments for two years in a row, earning the monogram of the college in both these sports. One of his dreams was thus fulfilled.

However, where he really shone the brightest was in uniform. He had joined the National Cadet Corps (NCC) in both school and college, regularly bagging awards for his performance. In the end, he was selected to attend an advanced leadership camp at Manali, in the summer of 1961.

During the training in Manali, Ashok and his other friends heard about an ailing old man who lived at the top of a steep hill and was unable to make the precarious descent to get to a hospital. A few of the young cadets, including Ashok, volunteered to rescue him. Ashok was tasked to organize the group and lead the way. They had to cross the river Beas, which was dotted with boulders, with the tops protruding out of the water, forming a zigzag of stepping-stones to the opposite bank. Ashok entered the river with the queue of other boys following as he moved from one stepping-stone to the other. Although they were slippery, the group supported each other and made it safely to the final section, a rickety, old, make-shift, wooden bridge. It was only after they arrived at the home of the old man on the summit of the hill that they realized he was too ill to accompany them on foot. Using some tree branches and rope, they improvised a stretcher for him and carefully carried the man down to their camp where they provided him with the initial medical care to stabilize him before moving him to a big hospital in the city.

With his tenure in college drawing to a close, it was time for Ashok to start working towards his ultimate goal—donning the uniform and serving his country. The Indo-China war of 1962 gave him the opportunity to do so earlier than he had expected. Since a national Emergency had been declared during this time, the NCC cadets, better equipped to rise to the occasion, were preferred over others to join the army as Emergency officers.

As soon as Ashok heard of this opportunity, he left for the Service Selection Board (SSB) in Allahabad without telling his family. He knew fully well that his family would not question his decision and would, in fact, be proud of him. He wanted to give them a surprise and left for Allahabad on the pretext of playing a cricket match, with his friend, Vinay, who also wanted to appear before the SSB.

During one of the SSB's gruelling physical tests, crossing a series of obstacles, Ashok stood first in the group.

Unfortunately, he hurt his hand in this exercise. The officer-in-charge ordered him to redo the final obstacle despite knowing of the candidate's injury. Ashok obediently completed the challenge, as always, ahead of the rest. Suitably impressed by this demonstration of will power, the officer told him that he had made the grade.

Although Ashok was selected, he chose not to celebrate his win because Vinay had failed in the selection process. Both the boys returned home. Ashok continued to keep the purpose of his visit and the result to himself.

Life back home had been carrying on as usual. Ashok had been consistently doing well in the NCC, but the laurels didn't stop there. His heart swelled with pride as he took part in the National Cadet Corps Rifle (NCCR) contingent on the Republic Day of 1963. He also earned the privilege of leading the then prime minister of India, Pandit Jawahar Lal Nehru, to inspect the parade at Safdarjung Airport, New Delhi.

Soon after, on a sunny, winter morning, just as the family sat down to enjoy their morning tea, an official-looking letter arrived. Mr Chattarpati Tara squinted in the sun, to read the document from the army headquarters in Delhi, noting that it was addressed to his young son, Ashok. Mr Tara was perplexed. His confusion and surprise were soon supplanted by pride and joy when he realized that it was a selection letter inviting his youngest son to join the Officer Training School (OTS) at Madras (now Chennai).

Ashok did not have to explain. He had given his family one of the best surprises of their lifetime and their happiness knew no bounds.

Nonetheless, Ashok, now in the last year of college, had to sit for his final exams and he also had to undergo the eye operation mandated by the medical authorities of the SSB before joining. This meant he had to go through yet another medical board after the surgery that would further delay his joining date. In light of his realization of his chosen path, these were but minor hurdles and he finally joined the OTS in April 1963, only slightly later than scheduled.

He was commissioned in the army six months later as that was the duration of the training required for the 'Emergency-commissioned' officers. Mrs Damyanti Tara's words had turned out to be prophetic. Her youngest son was indeed destined to become her 'fauji beta'.

4

On the Brink of War

The Government of Pakistan was fast losing credibility and also the faith in the hearts of the eastern side of the country. It was becoming increasingly clear to them that they were not being considered while making any decisions in the country. They had no reason to believe that the future would bring any change. The nullifying of their democratic election had been the last straw.

The people, especially the youth, felt insulted and angry and needed to express it. Thus, on 7 March 1971, a mass gathering was held in the Race Course Ground in Dhaka, comprising a group of restless and agitated people eagerly waiting to be shown the direction to the one thing they collectively desired—liberation. So, when Sheikh Mujibur Rahman, their very own Bangabandhu, took to the stage, all eyes were on him.

Their leader didn't disappoint. In one of the most iconic speeches of its time, that lasted all of nineteen minutes, Mujib called out to his people for independence, exhorting them to launch a campaign of civil disobedience. Encouraging his brothers and sisters to face the 'enemy' bravely and with whatever they had, he said:

> The people of this land are facing elimination, so be on guard. If need be, we will bring everything to a total standstill . . . Collect your salaries on time. If the salaries are held up, if a single bullet is fired upon us henceforth, if the murder of my people does not cease, I call upon you to turn every home into a fortress against their onslaught. Use whatever you can put your hands on to confront this enemy. Every last road must be blocked. We will deprive them of food, we will deprive them of water. Even if I am not around to give you the orders, and if my associates are also not to be found, I ask you to continue your movement unabated.[1]

He also laid down four conditions, under which the Awami League would attend the National Assembly to be held on 25 March 1971. These were:

1. Martial law was to be immediately lifted.
2. All military personnel were to be instantly withdrawn.

3. Elected representatives of the people were to gain power.
4. The number of casualties during the conflict were to receive a proper inquiry.[2]

An emotionally charged Mujib, famously ended the speech with these words:

> The struggle now is the struggle for our emancipation; the struggle now is the struggle for our independence. Be ready. We cannot afford to lose our momentum. Keep the movement and the struggle alive because if we fall back they will come down hard upon us. Be disciplined. No nation's movement can be victorious without discipline . . . Joi Bangla![3]

On the other hand, according to an article of the *New York Times* published on the same day, Gen. Yahya Khan had declared, just the previous day:

> No matter what happens, as long as I am in command of Pakistan's armed forces and head of state, I will ensure the complete and absolute integrity of Pakistan . . . I will not allow a handful of people to destroy the homeland of millions of innocent Pakistanis.[4]

For years, the people of East Bengal had been looked down upon by their western cousins for their docile nature and interest in arts and culture as opposed to more physical activities. They considered these a sign of weakness. Even after the passionate speech from their leader, when the crowds took to the roads in large numbers as a mark of protest, it was largely peaceful, barring a few reports of some of them carrying lathis and becoming embroiled in some violent incidents. People in large numbers marched on the roads, united in emotion and echoing the cry given to them by their leader himself—Joi Bangla!

In the days following the speech and after the civil disobedience movement had been put into effect, the Pakistani government slowly, but surely, worked towards the destruction of East Pakistan. On 15 March 1971, Gen. Yahya Khan, under strict security, reached Dhaka from Karachi under the pretext of holding negotiations with the Bangabandhu. They met the next day at the president's home, without their advisors and had discussions that lasted about an hour.

Following this, on 17 March 1971, Gen. Yahya Khan summoned Zulfikar Ali Bhutto to Dhaka and more meetings were held with Bangabandhu as soon as he arrived and again on 21 March 1971. By 20 March 1971, Gen. Yahya Khan had already met with the Bangabandhu four times.

It became clear later that these meetings were just eyewash, designed to distract the people while more and more soldiers poured into East Pakistan.

On 22 March 1971, Gen. Yahya Khan postponed the National Assembly scheduled to be held on 25 March 1971, citing the lack of unity amongst the leaders as the reason. On 23 March 1971, Pakistan Resolution Day, one could see more Bangladeshi flags fluttering on the rooftops of the houses in East Pakistan, as opposed to the Pakistani ones.

It was believed that the Bengalis could never show enough 'courage' to physically fight for their rights. Hence, instead of even attempting to resolve the issues and problems of its people through dialogue and discussion, the then president of Pakistan, Gen. Yahya Khan, chose to further suppress their voices and actions.

Yahya Khan quietly left Dhaka on the evening of 25 March 1971, refusing to listen to Bangabandhu's demands, while leaving behind orders for the most heinous acts. At around 11 p.m., the Pakistan Army became ruthless. Innocent civilians were brutally attacked and killed, helpless women were raped and countless houses were looted and burned down.

On 26 March 1971, Yahya Khan took to the radio to address the people of his country and not only denounced their (East Bengal) leader Mujib and his party, the Awami League, as treasonous enemies of the nation, he even went on to announce stern martial law orders in East Pakistan. As a result, a severe curfew was imposed. It was clear that they would rather force their people into subjugation rather than give any amicable discussions a chance, even though they had put on a show of attempting to do so.

The winning party of the general elections, the Awami League, was banned and its leaders, Mujib and his other colleagues, were arrested and taken to West Pakistan (where he was jailed) while Mujib's family, including his wife and children were held under house arrest in Bangladesh.

However, Mujib too, refusing to back down, made sure to address his people on the air even as the army started following orders and began its relentless crackdown. Signing an official declaration of independence of Bangladesh at midnight on 26 March 1971, he had it announced over the radio and told his fellow freedom fighters to create resistance against the army occupation.

The Pakistan Army was ordered to launch an operation known as 'Operation Searchlight' that was apparently aimed at neutralizing the militias that, according to them, were responsible for all the unrest and upheaval in the country. For starters, universities to hotels, nothing was spared as part of the said operation. The defence forces of the country were unleashed against the very people they were supposed to defend. Skirmishes broke out in various parts of Dhaka and Chittagong aside from the smaller villages that had been targeted earlier.

The marauding army stormed the halls and corridors of Dhaka University at one end of the city while on the other, Pakistani troops reportedly barged into the Intercontinental Hotel, tearing down the Bangla flag and proceeding to burn it.

The chain of events following these attacks were chilling. Although the beginning of the operation saw the troops targeting political leaders, doctors, students and other intellectuals, soon the atrocities spread to the innocent civilians of the province as well. No one was spared. Day after day, horrifying and numbing accounts of the torture meted out to the people of East Bengal came to light. According to some reports, any Bengali, alleged to be a rebel or even a worker of the Awami League was to be 'sent to Bangladesh', no questions asked, which was code for death without trial.

If, by chance, a young child escaped the prying eyes of the family's killers, it came at an unfortunate, deeply scarring cost. Witnessing the repeated rape of one's mother or sister before seeing them being murdered or the subsequent death of a helplessly bleeding parent became the new normal. Hence those who were spared could hardly be considered lucky. The nature of the crimes only became more inhuman and horrific with every passing day.

As Sydney Schanberg, the famous reporter of the *New York Times*, wrote at the time:

> . . . it was a surprise attack with tanks, artillery and heavy machine guns against a virtually unarmed population.[5]

East Pakistan became the land of cold, unforgiving terror and bloodshed.

However, Yahya's government had underestimated the people of East Bengal greatly for far too long. They had understood their peace-loving nature to be a sign of weakness. But the rise in the number of atrocities gave birth to battle-hardened and strong-willed young people, not much older than children, who were determined to fight back, in different parts of the country. A large number of them who also chose to take refuge in the neighbouring country, India, remained just as united in their will to fight for their freedom. As a result, there was a large influx of refugees in the Indian states bordering East Bengal, such as Assam, Tripura and above all, West Bengal.

In the initial days, the Bengalis on the Indian side, primarily in the state of West Bengal, who started to get exposed to the conditions of the people to whom they were connected by their culture and language (despite being separated by the border), were understandably enraged. The torture being borne by the people of Bangladesh received the harsh glare of the spotlight as several discussions and debates arose in various parts of the world, especially, as expected, in India. This crisis could neither be accepted nor ignored.

On 13 June 1971, the *Sunday Times* of London ran a sixteen-column (two-page) story, titled 'GENOCIDE' on the atrocities that were being carried out in Bangladesh, then East Pakistan. It was written by a Pakistani journalist, Anthony Mascarenhas, who had, in fact, been invited by the Pakistan Army to report on their operations several months ago. However, he could only have it published after he and his family moved back to the safety of the UK. The article, which he eventually wrote, was an eye-opener and a stunning revelation that shook the rest of the world.

Through the story of a twenty-four-year-old tailor, his article brought to the forefront the naked reality of the brutality that was being suffered by the people of East Pakistan every single day. This is how it began:

> **Abdul Bari had run out of luck**
>
> Like thousands of other people in East Bengal, he had made the mistake, the fatal mistake of running within sight of a Pakistani army patrol. He was 24 years old, a slight man surrounded by soldiers. He was trembling, because he was about to be shot.
>
> 'Normally we would have killed him as he ran,' I was informed chattily by Major Rathore, the G-2 Ops. of the 9th Division, as we stood on the outskirts of a tiny village near Mudafarganj, about 20 miles south of Comilla. 'But we are checking him out for your sake.

> You are new here and I see you have a squeamish stomach.'
>
> 'Why kill him?' I asked with mounting concern.
>
> 'Because he might be a Hindu or he might be a rebel, perhaps a student or an Awami Leaguer. They know we are sorting them out and they betray themselves by running.'
>
> 'But why are you killing them? And why pick on the Hindus?' I persisted.
>
> 'Must I remind you,' Rathore said severely, 'how they have tried to destroy Pakistan? Now under the cover of the fighting we have an excellent opportunity of finishing them off.'[6]

The article also contained details of the many conversations that he had had with several officials of the Pakistan Army which only brought to the forefront their inhumanly cold detachment towards the people they had been ordered to kill. In fact, the then prime minister of India, Indira Gandhi, told the then editor of the *Sunday Times*, Harold Evans, that the article had shocked her so deeply it had set her

> . . . on a campaign of personal diplomacy in the European capitals and Moscow to prepare the ground for India's armed intervention.[7]

Although the locals of the bordering Indian states, as well as its government, were sensitive and supportive of the conditions of the refugees, since as early as mid-April, the steady rise in their numbers became more than a country like India could handle. Despite the best efforts of the Indian forces and the government to provide for the refugees, the situation was getting out of hand. The resources of a developing nation, such as India, were limited already. It was clear that in the absence of a viable solution to the crisis in the near future, the repercussions of the turbulence in the neighbouring country would be felt on the other side in significant magnitude as well.

One of the officers involved in dealing with and taking care of these refugees was Major Ashok Tara. Even though he had been a part of the war in 1965, it was only now, seeing the state of the Bengali refugees, that he would be reminded of the time of the Partition, which he had witnessed as a child. Since his post in Dimagiri was opposite the hills of Chittagong, he dealt with the refugees directly. His orders were to provide shelter, medical aid, clothes and other necessities to the refugees.

Also, by now, the counter-insurgency (CI) unit, the 32 Bn Brigade of the Guards, to which he had been posted, had been redesignated as 14 Guards and converted to a regular infantry battalion. Owing to the political turmoil and resulting conditions in Pakistan, the unit had to train itself to fight a war as the weapons and training are different in a CI unit compared to a regular infantry battalion.

Meanwhile, the officers of the East Bengali Army as well as their police forces joined in the revolts. There was no one who could validate the senselessness of the brutal treatment of their people by the Government of Pakistan. Thus, in April 1971, these trained people in uniform as well as the agitated civilians, who had decided to fight back by picking up arms, ranged together as freedom fighters. They were eventually recognized as an important part of what came to be known as the *mukti fouj* (the liberation army). Furthermore, the people of Bangladesh who were politically involved and had narrowly escaped the Pakistan Army, also formed a government in exile in Calcutta (now Kolkata), headed by one Tajuddin Ahmad, who was a close friend of Mujib. It was then that the guerrilla forces, now known as the Mukti Bahini, gained more of a direction under the leadership of General Osmani, head of the military council.

Meanwhile, as the Indian diplomats in Dhaka had been sending back a series of reports about the atrocities and killings ever since these had started, news of the use of such brutal force on such a large number of people worried the already shaken Mrs Indira Gandhi. To her, considering the plight of the people of Bangladesh, it was clear who the Indian side was going to help. However, the sudden surge in the numbers of refugees made unlikely the possibility that the problem could get resolved simply by absorbing and taking care of the refugees, to say the least; India had to extend support in other ways as well.

Although a military incursion may have seemed like the only obvious way of extending support, such decisions couldn't be undertaken without proper deliberation. The time was not favourable for combat, hence, following the advice of top generals, including Gen. Sam Manekshaw himself, the then chief of army staff, Mrs Gandhi relented and agreed to wait. It was eventually decided that the Indian Army would help, support and train the Mukti Bahini known as the Mukti Yodhas in guerrilla warfare, to equip them with the skills required to effectively fight against a trained army, namely the Pakistani troops.

The Mukti Bahini had a lot to gain with the right training. Seeing the force with which the Pakistani troops were coming down on them, it seemed possible that they perhaps aimed to eliminate this armed resistance even before the monsoon season could set in. This was because the Bengalis, who were acclimatized to the inclemencies of the weather, were known to be masters of water. They feared that if these Mukti Yodhas survived until then, they would fight with an advantage that the Pakistani troops lacked. So, on the directions of Gen. Sam Manekshaw and the then general officer commander-in-chief eastern command, Lt Gen. Jagjit Singh Aurora, the BSF and the army worked in tandem and started the training of these freedom fighters in earnest.

Thus, the same orders were added to the charter of duties assigned to Maj. Ashok Tara's battalion. Now, in addition to providing for the refugees, the officers, including himself, had to organize a training camp along with providing weapons and field-craft training to the Mukti Bahini. This liberation army didn't have only young men—the training was taken by teenagers, middle-aged men and some women as well.

Regardless of their age, Ashok found that every single person, man, woman or child, held the same burning desire, that of fighting for their country, to protect their loved ones, to avenge the people they had lost and the one thing they all craved together—freedom of their nation.

Even though the war was against two different nations, or perhaps, more appropriately at the time, between two sides of the same nation, being exposed to its effects and the scale of human suffering it caused would often keep Ashok awake at night. When he looked around the camps—at old men, women and children—struggling for survival, it would motivate him to train the Mukti Yodhas personally. As the refugees desperately needed empathy more than anything else, officials like Tara on the Indian side could instantly evoke their respect and affections. Some of the women trusted them enough to show them the mutilations inflicted on their bare bodies by their own countrymen. It would make the flame of justice burn more fiercely in the hearts of the Indians. They vowed to themselves to help these people to the best of their abilities: they deserved to win, they deserved to survive.

This was truly the survival of the fittest for them. Those who had survived or escaped the brutalities had to weather the vicissitudes of the climate. Those who survived the weather had to survive the many illnesses that were part and parcel of the squalor in which they were forced to live. Thus, the road to a breakthrough was long and hard—the ones to survive had to be the ones who refused to give up!

5

A Soldier's Initiation

Ashok's journey in uniform started on 13 October 1963 when, as a young second lieutenant, he got commissioned in the Brigade of the Guards. Most of the young officers (also known as YOs) were first posted to their respective training centres, which in Ashok's case was in Kota, Rajasthan, in order to give them time and opportunity to hone their skills in firing all kinds of small arms. That is where Ashok found himself soon after wearing his ranks. The next few months went by in tactical training with arms, in addition to building camaraderie and to get a feel of the army from the grassroots by living with the men and participating in all their day-to-day activities instead of living in the accommodation normally allocated to officers. These early days are usually about getting a feel for life as a member of the armed forces. It is the time when close friendships are forged, and gives new recruits a holistic view of the responsibility of serving the nation.

However, within a few months, by the middle of 1964, he was transferred to the 3rd Battalion, Brigade of the Guards (3 Guards), situated then in Nagaland. During his short tenure there, he found that Nagaland was particularly sensitive owing to the active Naga insurgency in the area and it was normal to go on patrols that lasted for several days.

For an energetic young, twenty-three-year-old, recently commissioned as an officer, this posting turned out to be a great learning experience. This gave him an opportunity not only to do the work on the ground, but also to deal with the local population and civil authorities, which would help him develop the kind of communication skills that are imperative for any infantry officer. He would often be required to mingle with the locals and talk to the heads of the villages to collect crucial information about the insurgents and their movements, which in itself wasn't an easy job. But, with his miscible nature and pleasing manners, Ashok had a knack of making friends easily, so, in no time, he established cordial relations with high-ranking and influential villagers, thus making the task of overseeing the administration of these villages effortless and smooth.

It's no easy task having to mingle and fit in with people who, for ages, have been cut away from the mainland conversation. Besides understanding the fears and aspirations of the Naga people, Ashok had to open his heart and mind and build a certain level of trust between the locals and the army. At the best of times, people are naturally guarded around anyone donning an official uniform, but Ashok had a knack of being friendly, of putting his best foot forward and allowing strangers the space to feel safe around him.

Football also placed Ashok on a good footing with the youth of the village. His love for it had continued while he was in the academy. He had sprained his right ankle before one of the important marathons that the cadets had to run but the indomitability inherited from his forebears enabled him to not only complete it, but to do so with an excellent margin of time, to the amazement of his medical officer and other superiors in the academy. They say that language is a barrier that can be overcome by a mutual love for sport, and Ashok's love of football did exactly that. In the north-east, football holds a special place in the people's hearts and it became a common denominator for Ashok to form friendly ties with the youth of the area. Even in the villages in Nagaland, Ashok would often be found indulging in one of their most popular and one of his favourite sports, football, with the local teams. His amazing football skills had, in fact, made him quite popular with the young boys.

Over time, the local people took him to their hearts and started to invite him for their functions, which were more often than not musical evenings where Ashok always took an active part and engaged with his hosts. In his younger days, back in Delhi, Ashok had, once in a while, taken part in local plays and college dramas, so he used this experience to make an impression on his hosts and they thoroughly appreciated his performances.

That he enjoyed non-vegetarian food along with the local liquor or tea, was an added advantage in his quest to win them over as sharing the host's meal is considered a mark of respect. As the days passed, he blended well and became one with the natives. He was welcome in all groups, although he especially enjoyed engaging with the young folk. In fact, they even made him a part of their culture by teaching him to do their famous 'bamboo dance', which he learnt enthusiastically. Whether it was making his favourite dish or making local handicrafts to present him with, it was clear that the people of the village had also opened their hearts and homes to this young and boisterous officer. Ashok was a shining reminder that as a representative of the Indian Army, his job was to be as humanitarian as possible. His affable nature allowed him to do just that, and he cultivated a friendly relationship with the people within the bounds of his professional duties.

However, at the end of the day, Ashok was there for a reason and he never forgot that. He made sure to always be mindful of his limits and his duties as post commander. He was unfailingly polite and courteous but also forever alert and aware.

As the army requires the officers to keep up with their training by doing regular courses from time to time, by

January 1965, he had to leave his post at Nagaland to attend the 'Weapon Course' at the then infantry school, Mhow, Madhya Pradesh.

After three months, upon completion of his course, he returned to Nagaland, but this time, he was sent to another post, Kerong, which was on the Nagaland–Manipur highway, where his task was to ensure the security of the army and public transport.

He had barely started at Kerong, when a message arrived that he had to move to Imphal (Manipur), to participate in the Inter-Battalions Football Championship. There he realized that, after the matches/practice, there was plenty of time to both explore the city's local markets and places of interest and to meet with the concerned army and civil officials. He decided that he could also collect some information about insurgents in that area.

Thus, during one of his visits along with another army officer to a civil official, the ever-alert Ashok overheard the residents talking about a village, Chora Chand Pur. Their surreptitious whispering piqued his interest. He found out later that that village, located as it was at a junction on the international border of Burma–Manipur–Mizoram, was the hub of insurgent movements and smuggling. It was known for Naga/Burmese insurgent infiltration en route to Manipur, Mizoram and further on. If reports were to be believed, the villagers were also involved in facilitating the smuggling of drugs and other items.

So, one day, he decided to visit the village to explore and maybe glean some information that could be useful to the army in the process. Visiting these villages without a security detail at a time of insurgency was tantamount to entering a lion's den. Such civil operations are not unheard of, but Ashok had a different plan up his sleeve. He had grown up to be fearless and decided to go incognito. He travelled in civil clothes and by civil transport (contrary to army formation orders) without a protective team. Upon reaching the village, he contacted the local informer whom he had befriended during a football match in Imphal. Ashok met up with a few of his friend's close associates. He also visited three shops on the pretext of doing some shopping and explored the area, quietly observing the people. As he strolled around, he would make sure to stop near groups of people casually and chat with them, posing innocuous questions about the activities in the village.

As the evening progressed, he lost track of time and became late. Consequently, there was no public/private transport to take him back to Imphal. To make matters worse, he was advised by his friend to avoid civil accommodations as they could be dangerous for him and because he had come to the village without permission or security, he could not afford to get embroiled in any kind of a critical situation.

After much cogitation, his friend suggested that the church would be the best place to pass the night as insurgents did not venture into the church. Ashok agreed and spent the whole night in the church. He left the next day at the break of dawn. No one came to know about his visit to Chora Chand Pur. However, he had managed to collect and pass vital information to his headquarters for their action. They were impressed by his solo venture into Chora Chand Pur, notorious for its insurgency. Time and again, even before joining the army (and during his long tenure), Ashok was known to take his peers and superiors by surprise. He possessed a keen sense of intuition that helped him along the way. That coupled with the ability to remain calm and clear-headed allowed him to do things slightly differently than a lot of his peers.

Ashok returned to base. Soon after, while in Imphal with his unit, he was once again assigned to the mandatory commando course at Mhow.

During the course, a demonstration to cross a gap of more than thirty feet between two huge boulders was to be made to a team of officials visiting from Army Headquarters (AHQ), Delhi. They were visiting to inspect/assess the standard of training of the commando course. A commando student was detailed to cross the gap between the boulders with the help of parallel ropes. Suddenly, to the horror of the onlookers, the student dropped his safety belt and was left stranded, clinging to only one rope. It is extremely dangerous to move on a single rope without the safety belt. The student holding on to the rope seemed to be getting anxious. Ashok promptly volunteered to rescue his colleague and nimbly clambered on to the rock using a separate rope. He was carrying the spare safety belt and murmuring his oft-repeated mantra to himself, 'Fear is just a state of mind.' This was an extremely precarious operation because if either of them slipped or lost either their grip or their foothold, it would be disastrous for both. However, since he had decided to take charge, Ashok proceeded confidently, fully focused on the task at hand. When he reached the student, he managed to pull him up to harness the safety belt to the main rope and then bring him down safely. Everybody heaved a sigh of relief and the team from AHQ went back feeling more than satisfied with the ability of the commando students to successfully take charge during contingencies.

While Ashok was completing the course, his unit received orders to move to Ahmedabad, Gujarat, which was where he joined them after the course, in July–August 1965. Soon after, he went on annual leave for two months to see his family.

On 1 September 1965, while Ashok was still on leave, he decided to go for a movie with his family. It had been quite a while since they had spent time together and his folks were in high spirits.

After the movie, while coming out of the hall, Ashok bumped into one of his good friends, Anoop Singh. Anoop looked at him in surprise because he had just learnt of the declaration of war between India and Pakistan and the news had said that all army personnel were to report back to their respective units. Ashok rushed home to find out more.

On 5 August 1965, somewhere between 26,000 and 33,000 Pakistani soldiers of the Azad Kashmir regular force, dressed as Kashmiri locals, crossed the line of control and infiltrated various parts of Kashmir. This was a planned military operation by Pakistan known as Operation Gibraltar. The aim of this operation was to cross over to the Indian side and instigate the predominantly Muslim population there to rebel against the Indian rule. However, the apparently well-conceived, ambitious and multi-pronged military operation was poorly executed and fell flat on its face when the expected support from the Kashmiris didn't come, and instead, informers tipped off the Indian side well in time for them to launch a full-scale military attack on West Pakistan, leading to what came to be known as the Indo-Pak war of 1965, which lasted for all of seventeen days.

Delhi, where Tara was, was shrouded in a blackout. His father was out of town so, taking charge of the situation, his mother helped him pack his bags that very night and saw him off from the Old Delhi railway station. The train to his destination, Jodhpur, was to leave at midnight. Not bothering about the lateness of the hour, she stayed until the train left the station. She told Ashok to perform his duties sincerely, like a committed soldier and not to worry about anything else. She also reminded him that his father had been a part of an awful war himself in the Burma sector during World War II. She urged him to always remember that he was her 'fauji beta' a moniker that may have been coined by her but was now used by everybody around him. Smiling proudly, she assured him that she was very proud that her son was going to war and she wished him the very best of luck. Motivated by his strong mother's words and stance, he set out on his journey filled with vim and vigour.

By the time Ashok joined them, his unit had moved out of Ahmedabad. Although the skirmishes had commenced in Jammu and Kashmir, other areas of the country were affected as well. Ashok reached Jodhpur on 3 September and then Barmer in Rajasthan on 4 September, where he finally reported back. The orders for his unit were to move to an area close to Gadra City (which was also their objective) in Pakistan, while the Gadra railway station was in India.

Ashok's unit found out that, on 6 September, Pakistan had reinforced its posts in Gadra City, so the Indian forces also reinforced their side with a squadron of tanks (Sherman MkV) and an artillery regiment. The Indian troops were now ready to attack and capture Gadra City. Ashok, who was a lieutenant by now, was stationed as the platoon commander. As they observed the developments on the Indian side, the enemy started thinning out, but maintained a fusillade from their tanks. However, even though they were under fire, the unit steadily approached Gadra City to attack it.

Before the final attack, which was scheduled to be on 9 September 1965, orders arrived from headquarters instructing them to move towards Munabao railway station via Jaisingder railway station. Munabao was a strategic hamlet about 250 kilometres from Jodhpur. As Munabao had fallen into the hands of the enemy, the unit was now required to shore up its defences and counter their enemy's advance. The defence of Gadra Road was very important from both a strategic and administrative point of view.

This time Ashok was one of the platoon commanders with the advancing troops of the unit. He was ordered to bring the rear party from Gadra station to the advance base at Jaisingder railway station. In the early hours of 10 September, Ashok left Gadra railway station with the rear party in three-ton vehicles. After a while on the road, he heard the sound of enemy aircraft, which, flying at a very high altitude, could not be seen from the ground. Back in 1965, aircraft could fly high enough to be beyond both visual reach and firing range of anti-aircraft guns. (In those days, the equipment was of the World War II era. Troops had 303 rifles, with five rounds in the rifle magazine, as opposed to the advanced equipment being used today.) Normally, an aircraft had to fly very high and then nosedive towards the target to fire/drop bombs and then fly straight back up to its maximum height.

As soon as he heard the sound, Ashok immediately informed HQ, but was instructed to keep on moving and not be apprehensive. His mother's words ringing in his ears, he took the initiative and told the drivers to draw close to the high dunes and the troops to walk through broken areas along the road. Soon two enemy aircraft came down towards his column and strafed them, but failed to inflict any damage on either the men or the vehicles. They had had a narrow escape thanks to Ashok's well-timed, evasive manoeuvre and this was highly appreciated by his higher-ups.

Unfortunately, two vehicles got stuck in the sand dunes. Therefore, a third one was also left behind for their security and to help pull them out. Essential items were taken out of these vehicles and the advance was resumed. Ashok brought everyone on the road and moved towards Jaisingder railway station. The troops ahead of them had already reached Jaisingder and had secured an advance base to move to their respective areas on the high sand dunes.

The troops were deployed to dominate the railroad Munabao–Jaisingder–Gadra axis. The unit was instructed to engage the enemy by aggressive patrolling and organizing raiding parties. The enemy too would bring heavy (Hy) artillery fire when troops were under deployment. During the preparation of defences (which involved digging the ground), the forward troops had to bear the maximum brunt. Although it was hard and painful to witness the loss of his own men, a young officer like him could not have experienced war in a more authentic manner and learned lessons from it. This exposure to the brutality of war, that arrived so early in Ashok's army career, would stand him in good stead going forward. The realities of armed combat is the kind of experience that one cannot imbibe during one's training years. It is the measure of a man who manages to deal with the emotional toll of losing soldiers and still carry out the task at hand.

Finally, the unit carried out its tasks successfully. There was a time when, during the night patrolling, Ashok unintentionally went too close to the enemy reconnaissance patrol. In response, the enemy fired a two-inch mortar along with an 81 mm mortar from the main position at his patrol. Fortunately, due to the high sand dunes, both the attempts were ineffective and the patrol remained unharmed. Ashok accidentally twisted his left ankle and it got swollen. As a result of the injury, he had to be moved to the advance base, Jaisingder railway station.

Even though he was injured, there was no scope to rest in the middle of the war. At the base he had to ensure the security of the area. He decided to do so by getting fire trenches dug around Jaisingder railway station. Furthermore, in order to keep the enemy at bay, with the coordination of HQ, a train carrying non-combatant civilians was made to move with its lights on, to create noises and give the impression to the enemy that more reinforcements had arrived. It worked in their favour and the enemy stopped moving towards the railway station.

By the end of September 1965, after the intervention of external powers, offensive actions from both sides became very limited and there was more stress on patrolling or artillery fire than any major attack, culminating in the end of war. At the young age of twenty-five, not only had Ashok experienced and survived a war, he had also gained lessons from it.

But his tasks were not done yet. During the month of October, the process of a peace treaty had started between both countries as the Soviet Union had intervened and had asked both India and Pakistan to come to a peace resolution. Later, it was called the Tashkent Treaty, which stated that:

1. Indian and Pakistani forces would pull back to their pre-conflict positions, their pre-August lines, no later than 25 February 1966.
2. Neither nation would interfere in each other's internal affairs.
3. Economic and diplomatic relations would be restored.
4. There would be an orderly transfer of the prisoners of war (POWs).
5. The leaders of both the nations would work towards improving bilateral relations.

Although the treaty was criticized by both the countries, its political impact was more significant in Pakistan. Their leader, Ayub Khan, decided to go into seclusion rather than give his reasons for signing the treaty, which led to anger amongst his countrymen. The difference of opinion between him and Zulfikar Ali Bhutto about the treaty led to Bhutto's removal from Ayub's government and him creating his own party called the Pakistan People's Party (PPP). Furthermore, the Tashkent Treaty greatly damaged the image of President Ayub Khan, resulting in his downfall. It was then that he chose to resign as the president of Pakistan and invited Gen. Yahya Khan to take over the central government.

Under the official course of this treaty, some officials of the United Nations Organization (UNO) arrived at Gadra railway station (to be taken to the guest house, which was to serve as their residence-cum-office). Lt Ashok Kumar Tara was detailed as their liaison officer (LO) to coordinate their move as they met with army officers; he also acted as a translator between the civil authorities and the locals. As he had also been to a few troubled areas to ensure ceasefire and peace, he was the perfect man for this job.

The role of the UNO officials was to ensure that both countries were abiding by the conditions stipulated in the ceasefire. Meanwhile, at Munabao, one Capt. Ranvir Singh was designated to secure a post north-west of Munabao defences. While he was carrying out the order in the morning hours and reached the post to take over, the Pakistani side suddenly opened fire, thereby injuring the officer at the post. The news of this incident reached Tara who was with the officials at the Gadra station. He decided to take them directly to the post without wasting any time in arranging for anything else. He also figured that going with them would discourage the other side from continuing, or attempting, to fire again.

As he had hoped, as soon as the white flag of the UN was seen by the other side, they stopped firing. Tara and the officials with him spotted Capt. Ranbir, who was injured, along with another jawan, who was lying next to a well, while the others had taken cover. It was clear that the firing had targeted the area of 3 Guards. An officer was hit and hence time was of the essence; thus, in the absence of proper vehicles, Tara quickly evacuated the injured officer on camelback and took him to the MI room in the Paltan. Quick decision-making was one of the strengths that Ashok's experiences had helped him develop and fortunately Capt. Ranbir was successfully rescued in time.

Finally, it was time to move on. Ashok had previously excelled in his commando course and as a result, in January 1966, he was posted as an instructor in the commando wing, then at Mhow.

Ashok now had a chance to impart all the knowledge that he had gathered in his time in the army and during his commando course. He was determined to train fearless and astute commandos. In the training of commandos, survival of the fittest is the one principle that is always kept in mind. The commandos have to operate in all types of areas during battle. Therefore, proper training with all types of weaponry, unarmed combat (judo) and psychological warfare are all essential to make them mentally and physically robust. Commandos often have to operate behind enemy lines and in jungles for long periods; hence, they must also know how to survive off the land. Ashok turned out to be a model instructor because he relied on imparting practical knowledge to those in training. He didn't shy away from conducting certain tasks and methods on his own to show the batch-in-training exactly how things needed to be done. Even though he was pretty young back then, he had a commanding presence because of his varied military experiences thus far.

As is expected, several techniques are used for the said training. A commando pit (with a circumference approximately 50 ft to 60 ft and 2 ft deep) is dug to train them in unarmed combat. They are also taught to recognize edible plants and fruits in the jungle along with laying traps for small wild animals, capturing reptiles, especially snakes and making them edible.

To catch a snake, one has to carry a stick/branch of a tree with a V-shaped fork at one end. The v should have two arms, each about four to five inches long, widening out into an approximately three-inch gap at the extreme end. Upon seeing the snake, one must move close enough to wedge the v of the stick on the back of the snake's neck and then press down hard so the wriggling snake is unable to free its head from the stick. Normally, after making some sudden and strong lunges, it calms down. The next step is to grip it firmly by the scruff of its neck. The snake's poison is always in its teeth, so it needs to be decapitated; also remove four inches of the tail before skinning the snake. The rest of the snake is ready to be cooked and eaten like any other animal flesh.

In order to instil confidence in his students, Ashok would often carry out such demonstrations himself rather than leaving it to the men assisting him. This helped allay their fears. He was admired and held in high esteem for his hands-on approach.

After completing a rigorous but satisfactory tenure as an instructor in Mhow, he was posted to 9 Para Commando. This was a feather in Ashok's cap because it was the first para commando unit of the Indian Army. It was raised under the command of Lt Col Megh Singh, VrC, at Gwalior, MP. Officers and jawans with a commando aptitude, in addition to being physically and mentally robust, were selected from other army units to be a part of it, irrespective of faith, caste or creed.

After completion of the initial commando (Cdo) training, the unit (9 Para) was moved to Danasa, near Udhampur, J&K. While in 9 Para, Ashok Tara also completed his para jumps at Agra and took part in operational-oriented para drops near Udhampur. He was also a member of the selection team, which was ordered to visit army posts at Rajouri, Poonch, Uri and other areas of J&K to select jawans for 9 Para and also to familiarize himself with army operational areas. He continued teaching the digging of the commando pit along with the skill of catching and cooking snakes in his tenure with the para unit.

Ashok seemed to have had a knack of being at the right place at the right time, for within just the first few years in the army, he had been part of life-saving rescues, engaged in significant operations and had successfully undergone his own training and trained others in some of the most difficult exercises of an army officer's life.

6

The Battle of Gangasagar

By 17 April 1971, the government in exile of Bangladesh openly accused Pakistan of genocide (which was validated in June that year when a revelatory article by Anthony Mascarenhas was published with the same title) and formally announced their proclamation of independence for a sovereign democratic republic of Bangladesh. On the other hand, the numbers of refugees in India rose alarmingly and coupled with the monsoon weather, the overcrowded camps became a melting pot of disease. By as early as mid-May, the estimate was that the Indian camps had almost 20,00,000 people with about 50,000 adding to these numbers every single day.

It was often claimed by the people who had been a part of Partition that witnessing the unfolding of events was like reliving Partition.

The middle of the year saw the numbers of the refugees soar to around 60,00,000. Both India and Bangladesh could be seen imploring other nations to come out in support of Bangladesh. Gen. Yahya Khan could still negotiate autonomy with Sheikh Mujibur Rahman, thereby controlling the disaster that was now engulfing not just one but two nations together. However, Yahya Khan was not prepared to listen to any suggestions of peace talks with anyone.

The cold-blooded heinous acts carried out against the entire population of the eastern side by the government and military of Pakistan only served to harden the resolve of the freedom fighters to fight tooth and nail for the liberation of their nation. Men and women of all age groups were ready to endure any and every kind of hardship and fight back. Motivated by the rebels, the locals too ranged themselves with the nationalist revolution by seizing lands, torching wooden bridges and even cutting the telephone and electric lines to impede the work of the West Pakistan Army.

Meanwhile, the Mukti Bahini was being trained on the Indian side of the border. As the rebels from the army units of East Bengal had been trained as regular soldiers, they were prone to launching frontal attacks that invariably resulted in their suffering heavy losses. As Vice Admiral Mihir Roy, India's then director of naval intelligence, would say:

> . . . surprise was the most important thing, like making sure the attacks are carried out on moonless nights.[1]

Thus, the entire focus of the training was on training them for guerrilla warfare.

The officials on the Indian side were self-motivated in addition to being supported and encouraged by the government to help the cause of these freedom fighters of the neighbouring nation. Not only did they empathize with the freedom fighters' need for freedom from the brutal subjugation by their government, they also recognized that a free Bangladesh was the only solution to the suffering of the refugees, who were now spilling over to border states, where resources were being stretched to the limit.

> The army issues directives for motivation and for conducting psychological warfare by the regular soldiers, the guerrillas, the government functionaries, the Bangladeshi refugees in India, the people living in Bangladesh, and the Bangladeshi diasporas. It was decided that:
>
> (i) a large number of guerrillas must be inducted inside Bangladesh to strike at every conceivable place through raids and ambushes,

(ii) industries would not be allowed to run; their electricity supply would be cut off by blowing up electric sub-stations, poles etc.,
(iii) Pakistanis would not be allowed to export any raw material or finished product from Bangladesh,
(iv) vehicles, railways, river crafts and ferries which the enemy used for supplies to their troops were to be systematically destroyed, and
(v) after isolating the enemy, guerrillas would strike deadly blows on the isolated groups.

The Indian government's Ministry of Rehabilitation, along with the Bangladeshi government established special two-tier camps for young Bangladeshis . . . In the first tier, youth reception camps were established along various routes of entry about six to eight kilometres from the Indo-Bangladesh border for:

(i) providing rest and shelter for the youth after a long and arduous journey,
(ii) verifying their identity,
(iii) checking against infiltration by Pakistani agents, and
(iv) holding them for a few days pending admission into regular Youth Relief Camps, which were established in centralized locations.

The objectives of the second-tier youth camps were to:

(i) channelise and train the youths into organised and purposeful activities in service of Bangladesh on their return,
(ii) serve as holding camps from which the trainees for Bangladesh Armed Forces, regulars and guerrillas would be recruited,
(iii) train others as base-workers to supplement regulars and guerrillas.[2]

Maj. Tara's post was located on high ground on the east bank of the Karnaphuli river, which was the international border. Although, at the start, the liberation army lacked the skill that was required to fight the Pakistani forces, the burning desire to learn to do so was palpable. Furthermore, their understanding of the local terrain and topography made the trainer's job easier. Having seen the misery they had been put through, Ashok and his men left no stone unturned in preparing them for their impending task. He realized that, along with skills, they needed self-confidence in their ability to hold their own in battles with their enemies and so he needed to make sure that they did not face too much failure. Therefore, Ashok took it upon himself to accompany the Mukti Bahini twice, to support them and boost their morale while they crossed the Karnaphuli river in a sortie against the Pakistani posts opposite Dimagiri.

That India could have chosen to close entry to any more refugees was true, but, in view of the inhuman treatment being meted out to a large section of the population in their own country, denying them entry into the relative safety of the neighbouring land, was not something that the government could make peace with. As a result, in a few months' time, each camp had as many as 20,000 refugees and just one doctor (per camp) who could only attend for three hours a day.

In addition to the obvious threat to people's health at large, there was another looming threat to the Indian population residing in the border states as well. The overpopulation was putting intense pressure on the already rocky local economies, resulting in their collapse with the sudden inflation, which included spikes in food prices and unemployment: a debilitating burden for the poor. Perhaps the worst and more unaffordable, outcome of the situation was the resulting unrest leading to rising crime amongst the natives of the border states.

Although in the early days of support, the plan was to extend maximum assistance to the resistance forces just short of direct involvement, by July, the Indian government became convinced that, in the absence of a viable political settlement resulting in the return of the refugees back to their own land, India would have little option but to go to war. This decision had come about with good reason too: over 15,00,000 refugees had gradually moved out of the camps into the rest of the state. Also gradually, the issue wasn't just limited to the population of Bangladesh; it had reached India with significant effects, as the latter began to feel the financial burden of the refugee crisis.

Once again, as early as 21 May 1971, Sydney H. Schanberg from the *New York Times* reported:

> NEW DELHI, May 21—India's 1,350-mile border with East Pakistan is beginning to resemble a continuous and severely depressing gypsy camp.
>
> Vast waves of frightened and dazed Bengali refugees—India says the number has exceeded three million—have fled across the border to escape the Pakistan Army. Tens of thousands more are estimated to be pouring into India every day as the army continues its offensive, begun on March 25, to crush the Bengali independence movement in East Pakistan.
>
> Half the refugees are being housed by India in badly overcrowded camps, most of them hastily set up in schools and hostels shut down for the purpose. Others are staying with friends and relatives.
>
> A large number, waiting for new camps to be opened, are simply massed along the roadside—living in makeshift thatch lean-tos or in the open, unprotected from the monsoon rains, which have already begun.
>
> Some have taken shelter in the large concrete sewer pipes that lie at the roadside awaiting installation. Along some roads Bengalis who were well-to-do are begging.

With the massive daily influx, the situation is too much for India, a country with resources already strained to handle, though the Indians seem to be trying.

The sanitation problem is severe. Defecation in the open is common. Cholera has already broken out in some areas and dysentery and other gastrointestinal ailments are widespread.

Even in some of the camps where rudimentary sanitation facilities have been constructed, conditions have become squalid because of the impossible numbers of people. The stench in some camps is sharp and garbage is often strewn haphazardly.

From the condition of the refugees as they appeared this week during a three-day press tour arranged by the Indian Government, the Pakistan Army offensive has been much more devastating in human terms than the cyclone and tidal wave that struck the delta area of East Pakistan last November, killing hundreds of thousands of Bengalis and leaving two million homeless and hungry.

Though misery is difficult to measure or compare, most of the stunned refugees seem even more broken in spirit than the survivors of the cyclone because they cannot fall back on the will of Allah as the reason for their plight—as they have done through generations of deep poverty and annual natural disasters. They

> blame only 'the Punjabis'—the army is predominantly made up of Punjabis from West Pakistan—and because the disaster is man-made, they seem less able to cope with it.[3]

The situation in the months following the above report only worsened. By July, it was clear that preparations had to be made to be ready for any eventuality.

On receipt of orders from his higher authorities, Ashok's unit, 14 Guards, moved out of Mizoram and got inducted south of Agartala, Tripura, by the end of July 1971. They now had to undergo strenuous training to prepare themselves for the impending war.

In the next few months, while the members of the unit trained themselves and the Mukti Bahini also prepared for the war ahead, taking advantage of the situation, the Naxalites and the Maoist radicals started working actively in the refugee camps to spark a revolution.

Meanwhile, the situation in Bangladesh and India was slowly reaching the far corners of the world not only because the two governments were trying to appeal to the other nations to take a stand against the atrocities being committed by a country against its own people, but also because the people with the power of the pen, music and other creative mediums were doing their bit to spread the word and speak up against the actions of the Pakistani government.

Perhaps one of the most iconic events to have taken place during the time was what came to be known as 'The Concert for Bangladesh'.

One of the most respected and loved Bengali musicians at the time (who continued to enjoy the same level of fame for the rest of his life), Ravi Shankar was deeply disturbed to see the appalling conditions of his homeland and what his relatives were going through. Witnessing it all quietly was not an option for him. Sensitizing one of his good friends, the guitarist George Harrison of the very famous band, the Beatles, he decided to partner with him to plan a pair of concerts with the aim of raising awareness about the genocide going on in his part of the world as well as raising funds for the relief of the refugees.

One concert for the benefit of the victims of a country was an event held at a scale the world had never seen before. The first Sunday of August 1971 saw Madison Square Garden in New York city fill with 40,000 people, standing together to acknowledge the plight of the people of Bangladesh. Featuring some of the biggest names in music in the world like Bob Dylan, Eric Clapton, Ringo Starr, Billy Preston, Leon Russell and the band Badfinger in addition to Ali Akbar Khan and Ravi Shankar himself, both of whom opened the act, it was a grand success. As Ravi Shankar put it aptly:

> . . . in one day, the whole world knew the name of Bangladesh. It was a fantastic occasion.

For Harrison on the other hand, the famous writer of biographies, Gary Tillery, wrote,

> The Concert for Bangladesh sealed Harrison's stature as something more than just a major celebrity . . . He changed the perception of recording artists, making it clear they could be good world citizens too—willing to set aside their egos and paychecks in order to help people who were suffering.[4]

At a time of dire need, it was what the Bengali people were best known for that eventually helped them be heard at such a level: music.

However, the rate at which the people were being displaced outmatched any relief and support coming their way since, by the month of September, almost 80,00,000 (reportedly) refugees were now inhabiting the camps on the Indian side with no end in sight.

The middle of October 1971 saw Ashok's unit getting orders to move down south to Sreenagar, south of Tripura, where some of the Pakistani troops had moved. Alpha(A) company that was led by Ashok was sent to reinforce the post at Sreenagar. This post was held by Indian para forces on embankments as their role was to secure the road going along the international border between the two countries. However, the Pakistanis held a pond embankment, which was at a higher elevation than their post and dominated it with automatic fire. The intelligence on the Indian side indicated further consolidation of enemy troops in the area.

Thus, Ashok was instructed to establish a defensive position between their own post and the Pakistani post, located across the border and opposite their own. Alpha company eventually started moving to the designated area. As the enemy was on higher ground, the company's movement was visible to them. Surprisingly enough, even though Ashok's company was well within their own boundaries, the enemy opened fire, wounding one of the jawans of Ashok's company. Unfortunately, the exposed and barren stretch of land on the Indian side could not lend itself to providing proper cover. To prevent any further casualties, Ashok instructed his men to prepare defences by digging trenches and also passed orders for movement to take place only after nightfall. Subsequently, they carried out digging trenches for defence over the next two days, only at night.

In the meantime, the commanding officer (CO) of the unit, Lt Col V.N. Channa, heard about the wounded jawan and rushed to the post to take stock. Upon hearing about the unexpected aggression from the enemy's side, he was unhappy and expressed his deep displeasure, demanding immediate retaliation against the enemy. However, Ashok, seeing the situation and judging the circumstances from his perspective, suggested waiting for a more favourable moment. As Ashok was in charge of the post, his CO agreed to go along with his decision. Another officer, Maj. P.P.S. Kshattriya joined the company at this stage, to extend moral support to the officers and their men.

Fortunately, the suspense didn't last too long as there was information about the other side getting ready to celebrate a religious festival soon. Since, on days of celebrations and festivities, the other side was expected to have its guard down, it presented itself as a golden opportunity to the Indian side. They decided to capitalize on it and retaliate for the unprovoked firing upon them earlier.

Ashok called his 'O group', which is the operation group consisting of subordinate platoon commanders and their supporting commanders. Maj. Kshattriya joined them as well. A plan was put in place. It was decided that they would open mortar and medium machine gun (MMG) fire on the enemy at an appropriate time to be signalled by Ashok. This was to be carried out the next day when the enemy was expected to be busy with festival preparations.

As planned, the next day at dawn, when the enemy started getting ready for their festivities and were in an atmosphere of celebration, Ashok's company went on alert, waiting for his signal to open fire. But just as the firing was about to start, they discovered that, despite all their planning, things were most likely not going to go as scheduled. Subedar Ajit Singh, the 81' mortar-in-charge junior commissioned officer (JCO), told Ashok that the radio set was out of order. This was a grave situation because, in the absence of the radio set, there was no way for Ashok to be able to pass his orders to his men who were conducting the operation.

Refusing to give in to the setback, Maj. Ashok Tara devised an alternative plan on the spot. He declared that he would direct the fire by voice control. Explaining the new plan, he asked Subedar Ajit to position himself behind a tree, while the rest of his men were asked to form a (human) chain by placing themselves behind other trees and broken ground at a distance of approximately 100 yards in a row, until the last person was close to the mortar firing position. A code word was also assigned to denote the number of mortars to be fired, to avoid detection by the enemy. The code was *kabootar* (pigeon). Although it took a while for all the men to take their positions, as soon as all were in place, it looked like it could work. It lifted the spirits of the men behind the guns. Finally, Ashok placed himself behind some broken ground as well and got ready to direct the firing.

The new plan firmly in place, Ashok's company started firing and all hell broke loose. The enemy was caught off guard with only a few men on guard duty while the others were participating in the festivities in their civilian clothes. The possibility of regrouping to retaliate was nil. Soon, just as the Alpha company had hoped, the Pakistani troops raised a 'white flag' (a symbol to declare truce or surrender), simultaneously screaming out to the Indians to

Col Ashok Tara's mother, Damyanti Tara

Col Tara's father, Chattarpati Tara

A young Tara during his initial years in the army

Tara (second from right) with his fellow cadets at an advanced leadership camp organized by the NCC at Manali in 1961

Tara (right) at the Jaisingder railway station, Rajasthan, sometime during the Indo–Pak war of 1965

An artist's depiction of the battle of Gangasagar

Artist: Madhu Mansingh

An artist's depiction of the house on Road-18 in Dhanmondi, Dhaka, where Sheikh Mujib's wife, Sheikh Fazilatunnesa Mujib, his daughter, Sheikh Hasina, and other family members were held captive by the Pakistan Army in 1971

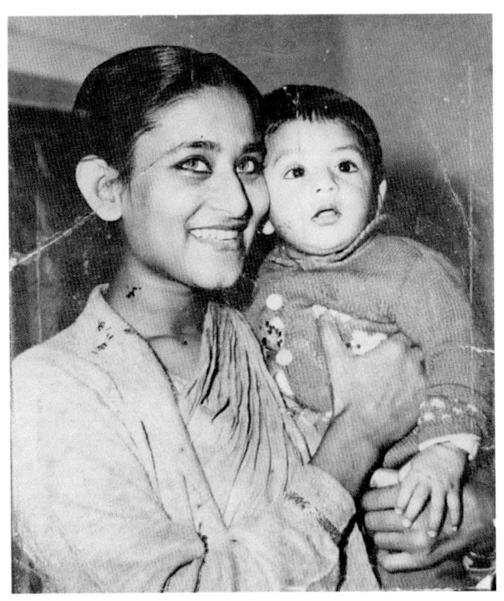

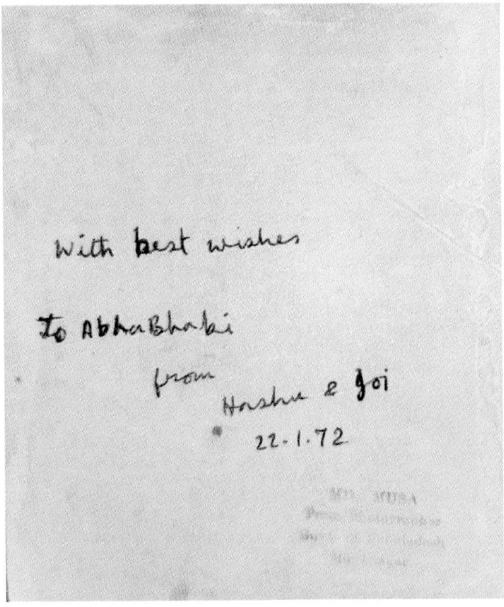

Photograph of Sheikh Hasina and her son, Joy, sent to Col Tara's wife in 1972. There was a short note written on the back of the photograph by Sheikh Hasina.

Tara meeting Sheikh Mujib's family and receiving a token of appreciation from Sheikh Fazilatunnesa Mujib, Sheikh Mujib's wife

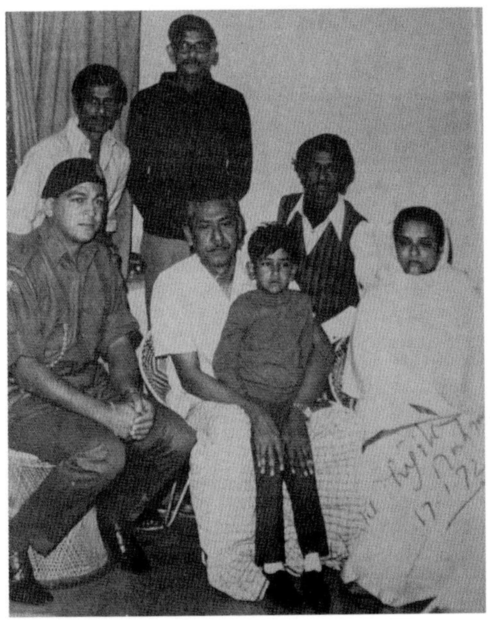

A photograph of Sheikh Mujibur Rahman's family with Col Tara (bottom left). Signed by Sheikh Mujibur Rahman.

Col Tara (centre) with by his wife, Abha (second from right), and Sam Manikshaw (right), chief of the army staff of the Indian Army, during the Indo–Pak war of 1971, at a felicitation ceremony

V.V. Giri, president of India, felicitating Col Tara with the Vir Chakra in 1972

Col Tara paying his respects at the Bangabandhu Memorial Museum in Dhanmondi, Dhaka, in 2012

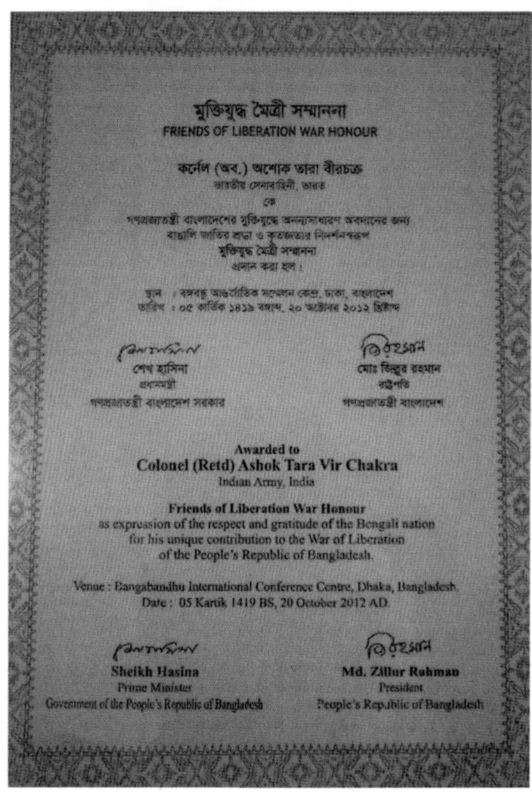

মুক্তিযুদ্ধ মৈত্রী সম্মাননা

FRIENDS OF LIBERATION WAR HONOUR

কর্নেল (অব.) অশোক তারা বীরচক্র

ভারতীয় সেনাবাহিনী, ভারত

কে

গণপ্রজাতন্ত্রী বাংলাদেশের মুক্তিযুদ্ধে অনন্যসাধারণ অবদানের জন্য

বাঙালি জাতির শ্রদ্ধা ও কৃতজ্ঞতার নিদর্শনস্বরূপ

মুক্তিযুদ্ধ মৈত্রী সম্মাননা

প্রদান করা হল।

স্থান : বঙ্গবন্ধু আন্তর্জাতিক সম্মেলন কেন্দ্র, ঢাকা, বাংলাদেশ

তারিখ : ০৫ কার্তিক ১৪১৯ বঙ্গাব্দ, ২০ অক্টোবর ২০১২ খ্রিষ্টাব্দ

শেখ হাসিনা	মোঃ জিল্লুর রহমান
প্রধানমন্ত্রী	রাষ্ট্রপতি
গণপ্রজাতন্ত্রী বাংলাদেশ সরকার	গণপ্রজাতন্ত্রী বাংলাদেশ

Awarded to

Colonel (Retd) Ashok Tara Vir Chakra

Indian Army, India

Friends of Liberation War Honour

as expression of the respect and gratitude of the Bengali nation for his unique contribution to the War of Liberation of the People's Republic of Bangladesh.

Venue : Bangabandhu International Conference Centre, Dhaka, Bangladesh.

Date : 05 Kartik 1419 BS, 20 October 2012 AD.

Sheikh Hasina	**Md. Zillur Rahman**
Prime Minister	President
Government of the People's Republic of Bangladesh	People's Republic of Bangladesh

'Friends of Liberation War Honour' conferred on Col Tara by Prime Minister Sheikh Hasina along with Nazrul Islam, the acting president of Bangladesh, in 2012

From left to right: Sheikh Hasina, the prime minister of Bangladesh, with Prime Minister Narendra Modi, Col Tara and his wife, Abha

Col Tara (second from left) with the wife (centre) of Lance Naik Albert Ekka, one of the casualties of the battle of Gangasagar, who was posthumously awarded the Param Vir Chakra

stop firing. As soon as the firing stopped, they requested an amicable discussion to deal with the situation. Honouring the request, the two officers, namely Maj. Ashok and Maj. Kshattriya along with two guards walked over to the border to meet a commander and two men from the opposite side.

As soon as they were face to face, the worried-looking commander of the Pakistani post requested that the Indian side stop their firing and in return, the Pakistani officer vowed, in the name of Allah, to offer no provocation from their end for as long as the Alpha company remained there.

It was a religious day for the enemy and a promise made in the name of Allah on this auspicious occasion was fairly significant. Besides, the Indian side had wanted to retaliate only to make their presence felt and let their enemy know that they were not to be underestimated. Seeing that the company had accomplished this goal, the Indian side agreed to back down. The idea of retaliating on the day of the festival may seem harsh on Ashok's part. However, Ashok's plan was simply to let the enemy know that any action on their part would not be ignored. In heightened situations like the one Ashok had to deal with, tough decisions need to be made and Ashok was ready to make them. On the other hand, he was not heartless enough to refuse a promise made by the opposition. Being a soldier, especially in a commanding position, requires more than just brute force. A great deal of empathy needs to foreshadow every decision and Ashok knew he had to tread in a manner that was forceful yet understanding.

In the meantime, 14 Guards (sans the Alpha company) returned to Agartala from Sreenagar in the later week of October 1971.

They soon received further orders to move post-haste to Dhalai (Kamalpura) to join the Indian Army units that were already engaged and fighting battles in the tea gardens in Sreemangal, Sylhet, since 27 October 1971. Sreemangal was situated on higher ground and overlooked Kamalpura. Since April 1971, this area had been occupied by Pakistani forces who had a Border Outpost (BOP) at the Dhalai tea garden complex bordering India. The area was covered with tea bushes and had paddy fields to the south of it.

While the post in Dhalai was a permanent Pakistani post, Kamalpura was on the Indian side. At the start of the battle there was an assumption that the post was held lightly. There had been raids conducted by the Mukti Bahini on this post, but they had turned out to be unsuccessful. It was only later realized that, contrary to their belief, it was actually a well-defended post by the Pakistani regular forces complete with concrete bunkers. Thus, capturing it would need suitable preparation.

The entire defensive area included a tea factory, Twin Hut, Red Hut and Coolie Lines. Several attempts were made to capture this area. Initially, the 61 Mountain

Brigade moved the East Bengal Rifles who fought valiantly, but unfortunately could not succeed. Then another unit, 2 Jat (with the same assumption of it being a weakly held post, with up to just thirty or so men) was sent, which also returned unsuccessful and with heavy casualties. Subsequently, 7 Rajputana Rifles were sent in and not only were they unable to make any headway, but their commanding officer, Lt Col Devasan, was wounded and had to be evacuated along with some other casualties.

Seeing the spate of failures and heavy casualties, Lt Gen. Sagat Singh (Corps Commander of the IV Corps) decided to take matters into his own hands. Since 2 Jat and 7 Raj Rif were already engaged in the thick of battle, 14 Guards from Agartala was brought in to support them because Pakistan had also reinforced its position.

By then, the battle was raging. On the one hand, Lt Gen. Singh ordered 2 Jat to dig into the Coolie Lines and defend against any counterattack by the enemy; on the other hand, 7 Raj Rif was supposed to capture Dhalai BOP. In the meantime, 14 Guards had reinforced their own troops to take offensive action at Dhalai.

The objective was to capture Twin Huts, Coolie Lines and Factory. Initially, 14 Guards, except Alpha company, had already moved into position and were joined by the Alpha company on the night of 1 November. Now together, the unit reinforced the defences of Coolie Lines and pushed deeper.

Once again, Alpha company under Ashok was tasked to capture the Factory area, one of the most sensitive objectives. Twin Huts and Coolie Lines were to be secured by C and B companies respectively. D company was held as reserve with the Battalion Headquarters (Bn HQ).

This time, with a well laid out plan and an adequate number of people to execute it, all the companies succeeded in their assigned tasks and captured all their objectives as per plan. Although the enemy, in a last-ditch effort, launched a counterattack; it was unsuccessful and the Pakistanis suffered some casualties as well. Unfortunately, during the encounter, a JCO, Naib Subedar Kanhaiya Singh, was injured along with one other jawan in the Indian troops.

Regardless, by now it was clear that the plan had worked and, after the arrival of 14 Guards as reinforcements, the enemy had started thinning out. Aside from a few last, but failed, attempts at getting at the Indian side, the enemy finally retreated in disorder.

By 3 November 1971, the entire area of Dhalai BOP was captured and secured by the Indian side. The morale of the officers and troops in 14 Guards was high and upbeat. Unknowingly, they had all been baptized for the impending battles they had to fight.

The Indian Army was now drawing up battle plans because it was evident that a full-scale war was unavoidable. So, the main force, IV Corps, which had the shortest approach to Dhaka, was summoned from the east via Tripura. 57 Mountain Division, a part of IV Corps, which was commanded by Maj. Gen. B.F. Gonsalves, was tasked to capture Akhaura railway station, opposite Agartala. 73 Mountain Brigade (of 57 Division), under Brig. Tuli was then instructed to capture Gangasagar railway station, 5 kilometres south of Akhaura.

The complex of Gangasagar was strategically located at a cross road between Brahmanbaria (located at the west of Akhaura), Bhairab Bazar, Kamalpura and Comila in the south, for being able to counter any attack/reinforcements to Akhaura railway station, which was the main objective of 57 Mtn. Division. Thus, capturing Gangasagar could provide the attacking forces a hub, which could act as a springboard for further attacks in any direction.

The initial plan of the attack was conventional. It was to charge at the enemy with armoured and artillery support. The objective was the Gangasagar complex, which consisted of the built-up area around the Gangasagar railway station, Mogra, Triangle and Goal Gangail.

The unit was ordered to move closer to the border and take position. The forward post deployed there made up for any lack of knowledge that their successors may have had about the situation and the surroundings.

When the unit started infiltrating through the enemy defences, it was through marshy and bushy ground. As the men trudged across the uneven terrain, carefully putting one foot in front of the other, the heavy weapons on their shoulders weighing them down, progress became slow and time-consuming. Just before they reached the village, Majhigaccha, they realized that they also had to wade through a pond, which was four feet deep and filled with water. But, with the help of each other, they managed to cross it uneventfully. It was a deserted village and as it was close to Gangasagar, the company commanders decided to assemble there.

The next night, a patrol consisting of Maj. Ashok Tara, Maj. O.P. Kohli, Second Lt P. Malhi and L/Nk D.N. Das, Hav. Girdhar along with a radio operator were sent to assimilate ground intelligence and enemy dispositions. The patrol, however, was unable to reach the enemy location, which was the Gangasagar railway station. Upon drawing close, to their surprise, they found that the enemy was well dug-in, with their defences reinforced with mines and wire obstacles. Furthermore, the surrounding area was low lying and marshy. The railway track lay on an embankment, which made it dominate the area around. This meant that a head-on attack, even with the help of armour and artillery support, would not be able to achieve their objective and in fact, would lead to a high rate of casualties.

While they were contemplating an alternative plan, the patrol noticed a handful of Pakistani troops pushing a rail wagon over the rail tracks. This rekindled their somewhat lost hope because it meant that the area between the rail tracks was not mined! Hence, if they were to approach their objective through this route, not only an attack, but perhaps even the capture was feasible.

This was exactly the kind of situation that Ashok, thanks to his commando training, was prepared for. He pondered for a bit and discussed it with the other members of the patrol party, eventually suggesting that they attack the enemy by moving along the railway track in a single file (column) formation. It was unconventional, but no one could deny that it could work. They all headed back to base and presented the plan to the CO, Lt Col V.N. Channa. On first consideration, the CO vetoed it on account of its being contrary to the original plan and unusual in nature.

Nevertheless, as Ashok and his cohorts understood their objective and had faith in their training as well as confidence in themselves, they persisted. Finally, seeing how sure they were, Col Channa gave in. But that was not enough because the higher authorities also needed to be convinced, because, as expected, the nature of the operation made them apprehensive too. To Ashok's advantage, since a second patrol also came back with the same observations and the company commanders displayed immense determination and enthusiasm, the higher authorities relented as well. The consent was given and the plan was on.

Permissions in place now, the battle of Gangasagar was ready to commence in phases. A premeditated assault plan was formulated:

Phase 1: Capture of Gangasagar railway station by Alpha and Bravo company

Phase 2: Capture of Goal Gangail and Triangle by Charlie company.

Phase 3: Capture of Mogra and Lilhat by Delta as a diversionary move to facilitate the attack on Gangasagar.

The troops were instructed to operate in total silence while attacking as taking the enemy by surprise was imperative.

Finally, at 2 a.m. on 3 December 1971, Alpha company led by Ashok and Bravo company led by Maj. O.P. Kohli moved out from the village, Majhigaccha, for the attack on Gangasagar railway station, while the others moved towards their objectives including that of creating the planned diversion simultaneously. Artillery support was on call.

It was dark and foggy when Alpha company moved along the right side of the track and Bravo along the left. According to plan, Alpha company was supposed to spearhead the attack over the railway track and take control of the railway station. Bravo company would simultaneously move westwards and clear the built-up area around the pond, behind and astride the railway station. The troops were restricted to a single file or column, on either side of the track since the railway line barely allowed a frontage of eight to ten feet.

Things were moving as per plan when suddenly Alpha company came into contact with the enemy's first bunker of MMGs. Ashok and Subedar Hoshiar Singh were leading the column and had steadily moved close to the first MMG bunker. They realized that the enemy had heard some sound of their movement because someone from inside the bunker shouted in a sleepy voice, '*Kaun hai* (who's there)?' This was met by Subedar Hoshiar Singh's curt response, '*Tumhara baap* (your father)!'

The enemy, realizing that they were under attack, acted immediately. They opened fire from one bunker on the Alfa and Bravo companies and critically wounded Sub. Hoshiar Singh. The Indian side was now exposed while the enemy was ensconced in a bunker and firing the MMG.

Acting upon his instincts, Ashok, without giving any notice to the enemy, quickly threw a Molotov cocktail and simultaneously lobbed hand grenades inside the bunker to subdue the enemy's offensive. Not wanting to lose the momentum and building upon his quick actions to avoid giving the enemy any time to recover from the impact of the two blasts, he grabbed the blistering barrel of their MMG and yanked it out of the bunker.

The place where the MMG had been was now an empty hole, revealing the inside of the bunker; Ashok saw two wounded, panic-stricken (Pakistani) soldiers, who had survived the blast, retreating. Picking up his automatic weapon in an almost reflex action, he shot them both down. Thus, within a few minutes, they had secured the position.

However, before the troops could attack and clear the other bunkers, the enemy, now fully aware that they were under attack, opened fire from their left, i.e., from within the built-up area behind the railway station. The element of surprise was now well and truly lost and the enemy opened fire from all directions on Alpha and Bravo companies.

Meanwhile, a section of the Bravo company, led by L/Nk Albert Ekka, had moved closer to the enemy lines, next to the pond area but they too came under heavy fire. Albert, who was firing and killing the enemy in the forward trench, unfortunately got seriously wounded. He was bleeding profusely, but, with total disregard for personal safety, he didn't stop firing and was hit a second time with a bullet. Oblivious to his physical pain, he continued his charge and ferociously targeted an enemy bunker located on the first floor of a building, by lobbing a hand grenade from a really close distance to ensure that it was completely destroyed. His act, although immensely valiant, resulted in his getting fatally wounded and dropping to the ground, thereby sacrificing his life bravely, while looking the enemy in the eye in the highest traditions of the Indian Army.

The assault by the Alpha and Bravo companies ended in hand-to-hand fights to clear bunker after bunker. The task at hand was hard, but the spirits of the men going in were harder. Finally, by first light, their whole objective, Gangasagar, was captured!

However, it came at a steep price and cost of the loss of some of the most courageous men of the unit. They suffered as many as eleven casualties. They were: L/Nk Albert Ekka, PVC (Posthumous), Guardsman (Gdsm.) Gulab Singh, Gdsm. Kashi Nath, Gdsm. David Tigga, Gdsm. Ram Deo Sahani, Gdsm. Udho Singh, Gdsm. Dal Singh, Gdsm. Kesar Dev, Gdsm. Malkiat Singh, Gdsm. Durga Prasad and Gdsm. Raman Bihari. Aside from the casualties, a total of thirty men of the Indian side were wounded, while Pakistan lost twenty-five of its soldiers to death while six others were taken as POWs. However, they were able to rescue their wounded.

The bravery displayed by the officers and the men of the Indian Army was suitably rewarded with some of them rightfully being decorated with bravery awards, including Ashok who was awarded a Vir Chakra for his exemplary courage and presence of mind. Four other people to receive the Sena medal for this operation were Maj. O. P. Kohli, Capt. Mahadevan, Capt. Mukhopadhyay and L/Nk Tilak Ram.

Ashok's unconventional plan was successful but the casualties of war are part and parcel of armed conflict. Ashok knew what he had suggested was dangerous but it was the only way the area could be captured. The exceptional fearlessness of those at Gangasagar that day will go down in history as yet another milestone of the bravery of Indian soldiers.

The battle was over; however, the war was well and truly on.

7

The Sparks of Love

It was the year 1968. Ashok was visiting his family on leave. This time, he had much to look forward to because everyone in his extended family was gearing up for a wedding and after his hectic few months at work, this was a very welcome break. One of his female cousins was to get married, which meant that this was a family reunion after a long time and everybody was excited. People were particularly happy to have Ashok during this time because his career gave him few or no opportunities for family functions. Thus, seeing him at this one came as a pleasant surprise to all who met him.

We sometimes forget that armed personnel have personal lives just like civilians. They are made to hold the affection and love from their families in one hand and the singular notion of serving their country in the other. Both these responsibilities have to be balanced throughout their long, arduous careers. It comes as no surprise that Ashok's family were always overjoyed when he was back home, and they wanted him to be happy, as well.

Ashok, by then, was of a marriageable age himself and although his parents were busy looking for a suitable match for him, he hadn't given the matter too much thought. Being a dutiful son, he honoured their wishes and met the girls whom his parents suggested, as and when they asked him to. He knew that the upcoming event was likely to give them a perfect opportunity to suggest more alliances because many young girls were expected to attend the wedding. Given his nature, he was mentally prepared for this even though he was probably not looking forward to it.

Weddings in India are an opulent affair and this wedding was no exception. The celebrations started off with a *sangeet* ceremony. This is usually held prior to the wedding and is a festive event enjoyed with singing and dancing in a casual and cheerful ambience as opposed to the more formal atmosphere of the wedding ceremony. Ashok too could be seen enjoying himself.

Being an extrovert with an ever-smiling face, his time in the army had honed Ashok's people skills to a fine point. He was comfortable in his skin and quickly established a rapport even with people he had only just met. He was enjoying the buzzing energy of the evening even though he was occasionally tasked with errands by some of the elders of the family. Ashok didn't mind and happily did their bidding with a smile. After all, who would know more about organizing events than a young army officer? After finishing one of these tasks, as he was returning to the group he had been talking to, he glanced towards the bride-to-be and noticed a pretty young girl, simply dressed, in the gaggle of girls around her. Ashok stood rooted to the spot. He suddenly realized he was staring and looked away guiltily. He rejoined his group of friends, surreptitiously keeping an eye on the damsel who had stolen his heart.

She seemed to be a good friend of his cousin, enthusiastically participating in all the rituals and activities. He couldn't help but instinctively seek her out for the rest of the evening. Her natural smile and beauty weren't lost on Ashok.

By the end of the evening, he knew that he couldn't let her go without introducing himself and getting to know her too. He waited for the crowd around her to thin out and then introduced himself.

They smiled at each other and Ashok shook her hand. She introduced herself, 'Abha.' She told Ashok that her parents were friends of his cousin's parents and that she herself had been the bride's friend for a long, long time. The conversation was interrupted when one of the others hauled Abha off to the dance floor to dance with the rest of the girls. Ashok couldn't help but notice how her smile never left her face. He watched her melt into the crowd before turning away, a big smile on his own face.

In the days following their chance encounter, Ashok found himself thinking of Abha often. Although he dutifully met with the potential matrimonial alliances presented to him by his parents and grandparents, no one could overshadow the impact that Abha had left on him. He knew her name, nothing more and was too shy to ask his cousin. He had no way of knowing how Abha felt about him so what could he even tell his parents? He was on leave for just a short while, so the rest of his days were spent daydreaming about that magical day when he had met Abha and wishing he could meet her again, somehow. But that was not to be and he returned to work without any decision in place although he had a much clearer understanding of whom he wanted to share his life with.

When he returned home during his next holidays, Ashok paid a visit to his maternal aunt one day. It was the same aunt whose daughter had got married during his previous visit, the time when he had met Abha. He had found out a little earlier that, like his uncle, Mr K.K. Sharma, who was an English professor, Abha's father, Mr B.N. Pal, too was a professor but of economics; they had taught together in their yesteryears in Shimla.

As Ashok drifted from one room to the other, meeting his relatives one by one, he suddenly came face to face with the one person who had been haunting his thoughts ever since their first encounter. His aunt, who walked past them, casually introduced them to each other and told Ashok that

Abha had arrived just a few minutes before him. It was as if all his prayers had suddenly been answered.

As the evening stretched on and Abha's house was some distance away, his aunt asked him to drop her home. Ashok could not have hoped for a better opportunity to strike up a conversation and get to know her better. Smiling inwardly, he readily agreed.

The distance between their houses was a thirty-minute journey on Ashok's scooter. Ashok made sure to have as much of a conversation as he could, for he knew he needed to know more about this girl who had occupied his thoughts for so long and wasn't sure if such an opportunity would ever present itself again. Since the discussions around his marriage were getting more insistent, time was of the essence.

Their short time in each other's company was all that he could have hoped for. He not only got to know more about Abha, he was now even more sure about having her in his life and felt confident enough to communicate that to her as well. A blushing Abha heard him out but didn't have much to say because she had been taken by surprise. However, her demeanour told him more than she realized and Ashok needed nothing more. As she got off his scooter and bade him a smiling farewell, Ashok knew that this time he was not going to leave the next meeting to chance.

But it was time to go back for now. His leave came to an end, sooner than he had hoped for and he left for his unit—this time on a good note and with a hopeful heart.

Back in the unit, Ashok made sure to stay in touch with Abha although, in the days when communications were limited to local dial-up telephones, letters and at most times just via someone who could pass on a message, it was difficult. But he managed as best as he could.

When he came home on leave the next time, he didn't want to waste time passing messages to and fro, as they had been doing for so long with a few short phone calls thrown in; he needed to see and talk to her to make sure they were both truly on the same page. He decided to simply go and meet her at her college.

Abha was a student of Miranda House in Delhi University, a girls' college and so, back in the day, special permission had to be taken to be allowed into the campus. Ashok knew that, given the fact that he was a young man who simply wanted to meet a student, he would not have a valid ground to seek permission. Ashok decided to take his chances to enter the haloed premises of Miranda House without official permission.

A sentry stood guard at the college gate. Ashok understood only too well that engaging in conversation with him would lead to unnecessary back and forth and accomplish nothing. Their exchange may even attract the attention of the other authorities in the vicinity, leading to his entry being denied. He decided to wait a safe distance away, out of the guard's line of sight, but from where he could observe the guard clearly. The minute Ashok noticed the guard's attention wander, he quietly slipped in and walked on like he fitted right in. He soon realized that he had absolutely no idea of the whereabouts of her classroom. Without stopping to ask for directions from the teachers and other students who were wandering around, he chose to keep walking without any hesitation, peering into the classrooms that he passed with the hope of catching a glimpse of Abha.

Fortunately, his plan worked. When she turned to see him standing at the door, she was both shocked and somewhat embarrassed. A quiet girl, she was not used to facing any unforeseen situation. Understanding her dilemma, Ashok signalled to her to meet him outside and left the premises as swiftly as he had entered. Relieved, she waited for the class to finish and then met Ashok.

By now, both Abha and Ashok were very sure that they wanted to be married. Their meetings had strengthened this resolution. Ashok knew that there wouldn't be anyone else for him and he didn't waste any time in communicating this to his family. Abha did the same and let her father know as well.

However, things didn't go as smoothly as the young couple had hoped. While Ashok's parents and the uncle and aunt who were friends of Abha's family were keen on the match, Abha's father wasn't. Abha's folks had had no previous experience of anyone who had served in the army and so her father did not want to condemn his daughter to a life which, according to him, would always have the threat of widowhood looming over her. He was, therefore, understandably reluctant.

The families did their utmost to talk him out of his fears, but the continuous pushing had the opposite effect on him. He grew adamant and became dead set against the proposal. It was a time when love marriages weren't as common, so he knew that his daughter would not defy his ruling. To ensure that he wouldn't get pressurized by others, he also tried to prevent Ashok and Abha from seeing each other. But the young couple carried on with clandestine assignations.

Soon, Abha finished her BSc and decided to pursue BEd. Upon learning of her decision, her father admitted her into Jamia Millia Islamia University, Jamia Nagar, Okhla, in New Delhi. She was required to stay in a girls' hostel and he figured that, due to the strict rules of a girls' hostel, Ashok and Abha's meetings would come to an end and, to his mind, this was the perfect solution to estrange the couple.

By this time, Ashok was posted in Agra. Now that he had moved and she had been sent to a hostel, they were unable to meet for some time. Abha's father's plan seemed to be working after all. Ashok decided, one fine day, that he could not and would not tamely settle with the cards he had been dealt and took matters into his own hands. He rode all the way from Agra to Okhla in Delhi on his scooter.

Once again, he found himself dithering at the entrance of a girls' hostel this time. He gave himself a stern talking to that, being an army commando who was doing nothing wrong, he had nothing to fear. Besides, as always, fear was just a state of mind; so, with the confidence of his training and his convictions, he decided to stroll in. Fortune favoured him yet again and no one so much as looked his way.

Even though he was meeting Abha after a long time, he was certain that he was not alone in his desire to spend the rest of their lives together. He was once told that 'lady luck smiles upon the brave', and it was perhaps his courage that made Dame Fortune smile at him.

This time their trysts did not stop. As he was posted closer now, he could manage to visit her more often than before. However, her father had firmly set his face against the alliance. Seeing the honesty and determination of the couple, the rest of Abha's family—her mother, brothers and uncle—now chose to bat in their corner. It didn't take long for the other relatives to join in as well, and soon, collective pressure was put on Abha's father to agree to their match.

To the surprise and relief of everyone, Abha's father finally relented. Without giving the couple much of a reaction time, he stipulated one condition that they should solemnize the wedding as soon as they could. Perhaps it was his last-ditch attempt to test the mettle of the young couple.

Hindu traditions demand that a priest be consulted for an auspicious date and so both the families consulted one at the earliest. He declared that the wedding could take place on either 3 or 5 October, as 4 October was deemed inauspicious.

Ashok and his family, who had no place for superstition in their lives or for this event, shunned these notions and chose to decide upon a date that would be convenient for their friends and family. They believed more in the blessings and best wishes of their loved ones for the new couple and their life ahead than what their 'stars' had to say. So, as 4 October was a Saturday, which meant most of his unit officers could be there for the ceremony, Ashok decided to go ahead with that date.

The wedding had to take place in an Arya Samaj mandir as the notice was short and making arrangements in other venues would have taken an inordinate amount of time.

This suited Ashok. All he wanted was to be wedded to the woman he had chosen. So, on 4 October 1970, dressed in a smart black suit and a striking red-and-gold saree respectively, Ashok and Abha tied the knot in a simple ceremony after an uphill struggle and a courtship of almost two years. The wedding was followed by a reception the very next day at the Constitution Club of India in Delhi where the newly wedded couple happily met and accepted the blessings of their extended family and well-wishers. Their happiness was reflected in their broad smiles throughout the evening.

Ashok had won the battle of love successfully but soon after, the call of duty started knocking at his door. Ashok left his new bride with his parents in Delhi and set out in the service of his first love—his nation.

8

Col Tara: The Lone Wolf

While the Indian Army was busy helping the people of Bangladesh to survive and be better equipped for their war of liberation, it was business as usual for the rest of the country.

On 3 December 1971, Mrs Gandhi, the prime minister of India, was on a visit to Calcutta and all seemed quiet and normal in the capital city of India, Delhi. A little before 6 p.m., people were flabbergasted when deafening raid sirens rent the air.

At approximately 5.30 p.m. on 3 December 1971, Pakistan had once again taken the world, especially India, by surprise and had launched coordinated air strikes by its air force on crucial airfields in the northern parts of India—Punjab, Rajasthan and Uttar Pradesh.

There was no beating about the bush any more as the leaders of both the countries formally announced that they were at war. While Mrs Gandhi chose to announce it over the radio on the night of 3 December 1971, Gen. Yahya Khan declared it on 4 December 1971. The *New York Times* carried Mrs Gandhi's detailed statement on 4 December 1971.

> I speak to you at a moment of grave peril to our country and our people. Some hours ago, soon after 5:30 P.M. on Dec. 3, Pakistan launched a full-scale war against us.
>
> The Pakistan Air Force suddenly struck at our airfields in Amritsar, Pathankot, Srinagar, Avantipur, Utterlai, Jodhpur, Ambala and Agra.
>
> Their ground forces are shelling our defence positions in Sulemankhi, Khemkaran, Poonch and other sectors.
>
> Since last March we have borne the heaviest of burdens and withstood the greatest of pressure and a tremendous effort to urge the world to help in bringing about a peaceful solution, in preventing annihilation of an entire population whose only crime was to vote democratically.
>
> But the world ignored the basic causes and concerned itself only with certain repercussions.
>
> The situation was bound to deteriorate, and the courageous band of freedom fighters have been staking their all in defence of the values for which we also have struggled and which are basic to our way of life.

> Today, the war in Bangladesh has become a war on India, and this imposes upon me, my Government and the people of India an awesome responsibility. We have no other option but to put our country on a war footing. Our brave officers and jawans are at their posts, mobilized for the defence of the country. Emergency has been declared for the whole of India. Every necessary step is being taken, and we are prepared for any eventualities.
>
> I have no doubt that it is the united will of our people that this wanton and unprovoked aggression of Pakistan should be decisively and finally repelled. In this resolve, the Government is assured of the full and unflinching support of all political parties and every Indian citizen.
>
> We must be prepared for a long period of hardship and sacrifice. We are peace loving people, but we know that peace cannot last if we do not guard our freedom, our democracy and our way of life. So today we fight, not merely for territorial integrity, but for the basic ideals which have given strength to this country, and in this alone we can progress to a better future. Aggression must be met and the people of India will meet it with fortitude and determination, with discipline and the utmost unity.'[1]

On the night of 4 December 1971, India retaliated with a multi-pronged assault on Dhaka. Two days later,

Mrs Gandhi announced India's recognition of Bangladesh as an independent nation to thunderous applause in Parliament.

Meanwhile, even though the fight was on the eastern side, Pakistan used the conflict as an opportunity to try and gain a lead in Kashmir, to compensate for the losses on their eastern front, by pushing their troops to create disturbances along the line of control. However, the Indian defence forces were anything but unprepared. As the then chief of army staff, Gen. Sam Manekshaw, famously told the officer, who had rushed to him to inform him about the attack,

> Don't look so scared, sweetie. Do I look worried?[2]

A few days following the attacks, effects of the tensions on the borders spilled over into the interiors of India as the Government of India imposed nightly blackouts in the city, while encouraging the civilians to dig trenches in order to avoid being targeted by the enemy's fighter aircraft overhead, which needed to identify their targets visually before bombing them. These measures were to minimize outdoor light and prevent enemy aircraft from being able to identify their targets by sight. At night, when the siren was sounded, people would voluntarily switch off all lights. The blackout would end after an all-clear siren was sounded. Whether there really was an air raid or not, it was an exercise for the citizens to be alert because one could never know.

Since one of the airfields that was attacked was Agra, even the Taj Mahal had been covered with burlap and camouflaged with a forest of twigs and leaves, because otherwise its marble would shine like a white beacon in the moonlight at night.

Months upon months had passed, trying to resolve the situation by urging Pakistan (and other countries to support the cause) to release the elected leader of Bangladesh and to discuss and reconcile their issues internally. It was now clear that this problem was only going to be settled at the end of this war. Thus, the days following the attack saw Indian troops, supported by the Mukti Bahini, both fighting equally bravely and giving their all in service of their respective nations against a common enemy. There were times when the locals in Bangladesh would also do their bit by helping the Indian Army push and transport heavy weapons across the boggy rice fields while their friends carried the ammunition. Their knowledge about the terrain and the best routes within their country came in handy.

The intention of the Indian forces was clear. On the east, it was to capture Dhaka and on the west, it was to prevent the Pakistani forces from entering India. The troops of both sides were now, with no exception, clearly in the thick of war. They would carry photographs of their wives, children or their deity to stay motivated to go back home and have faith in achieving victory. In most areas, the firing would often start in the afternoon and keep going long after midnight.

A few days into the war, the Pakistan Army started crumbling in the east. Thus, as the thirteen-day war approached its end, the Indian side often urged the enemy troops to surrender rather than die. However, that would often be met with refusal, as one Pakistani colonel wrote in his letter,

> Give my love to the Muktis . . .[3]

enclosing a Chinese-made bullet in reply. However, Gen. Manekshaw continued to insist on employing the tactic as he broadcasted repeated appeals, asserting that the POWs would be treated honourably according to the Geneva convention.

Meanwhile, 14 Guards, after the battle of Gangasagar, was ordered to move towards Bharam Bazaar. Aside from minor resistance at a few places, the unit landed in Markua at the end of a forced march of eight hours, uneventfully. After a while, the unit observed a Pakistani contingent consisting of approximately thirty armed personnel walking back from the direction of Pubail, which was on the northwest of Markua, to fall back to Tungi, the 'Gateway to Dhaka'. The 'D' and 'C' companies of the unit were in the forward position when the enemy noticed their movement and started firing at them.

In response, the Alpha company, under Maj. Ashok Tara, was ordered to encircle them so they could not escape, while they (the enemy) fired and simultaneously ran towards a deserted house for cover and a safe firing position. Troops in location immediately got into action, chasing after and simultaneously encircling the enemy as they ran towards their place of hiding. Both sides kept up their firing as they ran. One Indian officer, Capt. Ram Kumar, and a jawan were wounded in the crossfire. The enemy could not sustain their resistance after some hand grenades were lobbed into their hideout and their firing subsided abruptly.

After waiting for a few minutes to ensure the fusillade didn't suddenly start again, the unit personnel of 14 Guards entered the house where the enemy was hiding. Sure enough, they found a few dead bodies and six survivors who were cowering behind pieces of furniture that were strewn about in the room. Realizing that they were cornered, these survivors promptly raised their hands in surrender. Approximately thirty small arms of all sorts were also captured. The rest of the Pakistanis had withdrawn to Dhaka.

Thus, the capture of Markua/Tungi came to be known as the Gateway to Dhaka. On the eve of 15–16 December, the Alpha and Bravo companies of 14 Guards, moving under the command of Maj. Tara and Maj. O.P. Kohli, respectively, led the march of the unit to Dhaka. Subsequently, on the same night, both companies secured Dhaka airport and captured it by the morning of 16 December 1971.

The Indian Army had now surrounded Dhaka and eventually issued a thirty-minute window as an ultimatum to the Pakistani forces to surrender on 16 December 1971. Left with no other option, the commander of the Pakistani Eastern Command, Lt Gen. A.A.K. Niazi conceded without putting up any resistance, thereby bringing about the collapse of the Pakistani government in Bangladesh. Following this, a unilateral ceasefire was declared as Pakistan surrendered its entire military to the Indian Army, when the instrument of surrender was signed between Lt Gen. Jagjit Singh Aurora, the GOC-in-C of Indian Eastern Command and Lt Gen. A.A.K. Niazi, the commander of the Pakistan Eastern Command, at the Ramna Race Course in Dhaka at 1631 hours IST on 16 December 1971, marking the end of the thirteen-day-long war and thereby confirming the Independence of Bangladesh.

While the surrender was offered tearfully by Lt Gen. Niazi, it was accepted silently by Lt Gen. Aurora. However, the general crowd created a hostile environment by shouting anti-Pakistan slogans and abusing the surrendering army.

An article in the *New York Times*, carrying the surrender statement by Mrs Gandhi, on the next day stated:

> I have an announcement to make which I think the House has been awaiting for some time. The West Pakistani forces have unconditionally surrendered.
>
> Dacca is now the free capital of a free country.
>
> The instrument of surrender was signed at Dacca at 4:31 P.M. by Lieut. Gen. A.A.K. Niazi on behalf of Pakistan Eastern Command, and Lieut. Gen. Jagjit Singh Aurora. commander in chief of Indian and Bangladesh forces in the eastern theater, accepted the surrender.
>
> This House and the entire nation rejoice in this historic event.,
>
> 'Quality and Capacity'
>
> We hail the people of Bangladesh in their hour of triumph. We hail the brave young men and boys of the Mukti Bahini for their valor and dedication.
>
> We are proud of our own army, navy, air force and the border security force, who have so magnificently demonstrated their quality and capacity.
>
> Their discipline and devotion to duty are well known. India will remember with gratitude the sacrifices of those who have laid down their lives, and our thoughts are with their families.
>
> Our armed forces are under strict orders to treat Pakistani prisoners of war in accordance with the

Geneva Convention and to deal with all sections of the population of Bangladesh in a humane manner.

Indian Objectives Listed.

The commanders of the Mukti Bahini have issued similar orders to their forces.

Although the government of Bangladesh has not yet been given the opportunity to sign the Geneva Convention, they also have declared that they will fully abide by it.

It will be the responsibility of the government of Bangladesh, Mukti Bahini and the Indian armed forces to prevent any reprisals.

Our objectives were limited—to assist the gallant people of Bangladesh and their Mukti Bahini to liberate their country from a reign of terror and to resist aggression on our own land. The Indian armed forces will not remain in Bangladesh any longer than is necessary.

The millions who were driven out of their homes across our borders have already begun trekking back. The rehabilitation of this war-torn land calls for dedicated teamwork by its government and people.

We hope and trust that the father of this new nation, Sheik Mujibur Rahman, will take his rightful place among his own people and lead Bangladesh to peace, progress and prosperity. The time has come when they can together look forward to a meaningful

> future in their Sonar Bangla [Golden Bengal]. They have our good wishes.
>
> The triumph is not theirs alone. All nations who value the human spirit will recognize it as a significant milestone in man's quest for liberty.[4]

Pratap Bhanu Mehta, a leading Indian scholar and analyst, later wrote:

> India's 1971 armed intervention in East Pakistan, undertaken for a mixture of reasons, is widely and fairly regarded as one of the world's most successful cases of humanitarian intervention against genocide.

What was now left to do was to control events such as the crowd's hostility and the restoration of law and order in the city. By the early hours of 17 December 1971, 14 Guards had implemented all relevant protocols to secure the perimeter. However, on the same day, around 9 a.m., while Ashok was busy reassessing the arrangements with one Maj. Shanti Khanna, he was hastily summoned by his commanding officer, Lt Col V.N. Channa. Not expecting anything serious, as the unit had finally heaved a huge sigh of relief, Ashok assumed he may want to speak to him about the security arrangements of the departing officials and hurried over to meet him.

When he was in front of the CO, he was slightly surprised to see a Mukti Bahini yodha standing beside him. As his CO did not seem particularly worried (since he did not realize the gravity of the situation), Ashok had no reason to expect what he learnt next. The yodha informed them that the family of their Bangabandhu—his wife and children, including his daughter, Sheikh Hasina—had been held hostage by a contingent of the enemy troops since March and were still not released. The Bangabandhu was also yet to be released by the Pakistan Army.

The Mukti Bahini yodha, however, did not emphasize either the sensitivity of the situation or the need for immediate action with appropriate preparation, for there was a potential threat to the lives of the imprisoned family members who could be assassinated at any time. Therefore, assuming that it was merely a matter of negotiation as the Pakistan Army had already surrendered, the CO asked Ashok to go along with the informer and take just two guardsmen with him.

Thus, with the yodha as his guide and the guardsmen as his support to what he didn't yet know was going to be a dangerous rescue mission, Ashok arrived at the place where the first family of Bangladesh had been in captivity.

Upon reaching a distance of about 100 yards from the house, Ashok sensed that the situation was not as easy as they had assumed. A crowd had gathered and the people looked nervous, speaking to each other in hushed whispers and occasionally pointing towards the house before them. Upon questioning, the locals around the house told Ashok that the soldiers guarding the house were oblivious of the fact that the war had come to an end and were, therefore, still trigger-happy and ready to deal with any offensive situation with their enemy in the same spirit as before. They were also in possession of automatic weapons and would not hesitate to use them. To make sure he understood the extreme sensitivity of the situation and the import of their words, they directed his attention towards a bullet-ridden car with a dead body weltering in a pool of blood, which belonged to a reporter who had been trying to gather information about the after effects of the recently ended war. As Ashok took in the chilling message conveyed by the car and the corpse in it, the crowd once again requested him to carefully re-evaluate his approach as it was only the three of them from the Indian Army and for all they knew (due to lack of any clear information) they could easily be outnumbered by the enemy guarding the premises inside.

The seriousness of the situation was as clear as day by now and the odds significantly not in their favour. Ashok took a step back to pause and analyse the situation. It was apparent that his resources were limited as compared to a well-entrenched enemy, comfortably ensconced behind sandbagged bunkers that had been placed above and around the house. As he looked at the house trying to get a clearer picture, he realized that it looked less like a house and more like an enemy fortification as the people guarding the house had converted practically every corner into a small enemy bunker, with nozzles of guns protruding from little windows near the straw roof and sandbags all around the bottom of the house. The only visible feature beyond the iron gates of the house was a window on the front wall of the house, but it was too far to be able to discern anyone within. On further discussion, it became clear that there were around ten to twelve guards so they most definitely outnumbered the Indian contingent of three; and furthermore, they had more effective weapons, hence the option of bulldozing their way through and rescuing the hostages was off the table.

The other obvious option was to call for backup, but that had its limitations too because it would only lead to added queries about the situation and the reinforcement would take time to arrive, leaving the family in the custody of the enemy and endangered for a longer time. Besides, even then, any blatant charge spelled potential risk to the life of the family as the trigger-happy enemy soldiers could simply shoot them out of panic.

The only thing that was clear to Ashok was that the task had to be done quickly as time was of the essence. For a moment, he reverted to his commando-training days, hoping to come up with a solution to this conundrum. He remembered that sometimes battles were not just won by weapons, they needed a 'present' mind.

In a moment, his decision was made. He decided to take his chances and tackle the situation psychologically, by talking the enemy into surrendering. All things considered, he decided that was his best option to successfully rescue the first family of the new country of Bangladesh, or at least attempt to do so. He decided to go in unarmed!

However, Ashok was also a realist and knew that his approach was unconventional and that his chances of success were slim. He decided that he could not risk the lives of his jawans in addition to his own. Handing over his weapon to one of them, he instructed them to position themselves with their weapons at vantage points outside the house, using their own judgement and to be ready for any contingency.

Within the next few minutes, one unarmed officer of the 14 Guards, Maj. Ashok Tara, braced himself to take on one of the most difficult, yet significant, steps of his life, towards a house full of armed enemies. As he neared the entrance, his heart beat faster. He had to go past the bullet-ridden car. One slow, but mindful, step after the other and he was at the location of the car. Reminding himself of his father's words 'fear is a state of the mind', he decided to start his rendezvous with the enemy, as he confidently called out, '*koi hain* (anybody there)?' A question that was met with an eerie silence.

Cautiously, he kept moving forward, keeping a stoic expression and inwardly reminding himself to remain calm. When he was just ten yards from the main entrance, he finally heard a Pakistani soldier shout back at him, from atop the house, in Punjabi. He asked him to stop where he was or expect retaliating fire. There was no confusion in Ashok's understanding of these words as Ashok was well versed in the language he spoke and understood equally well that he meant every word. He could feel the gravity of the threat in his bones.

That he was now in the thick of things was not lost on Ashok, so he proceeded to respond in the same language (to establish a rapport), apprising them that he was an officer of the Indian Army, as they could figure out from his uniform. He urged them to understand that he was standing before them, unarmed, which was only possible because the Pakistan Army had already surrendered and the war, which they all had been a part of, was now over.

This was news to them, but hearing of it from an Indian Army officer, who was supposed to be the enemy, they were unconvinced. They even said, 'The Pakistan Army would never surrender.' Fortunately for Ashok, at that very instant, an Indian Army helicopter flew overhead. He grabbed the godsend and re-conveyed the information to them, citing the overhead helicopter as an example of the surrender, because, how else could an Indian chopper make an unimpeded flight in the skies of enemy territory? He reiterated that this was possible only because the Indian Army was in control of the capital city.

This struck a chord with the enemy. They seemed confused and asked for some time to speak to their commanders. However, using his commando instincts, Ashok knew that he had to maintain the flow of conversation with the soldier without giving him time to perform any other action, so he re-asserted that since all the officers of the Pakistan Army were now POWs and their communication grid was offline, they would not be able to speak to anyone.

The entire time that Ashok was conversing with the enemy on the roof, he was also steadily pacing himself towards the soldier positioned at the front gate, since his end goal was to enter the house. Suddenly a woman inside the house started waving frantically at him through the window he had noticed earlier, crying, 'Do not trust these men! They are very happy to shoot and kill anyone!' Ashok's fears of the intentions of the enemy were now reconfirmed, but he decided to keep going, without giving them any time to consider alternatives and continued to convince them to capitulate. Meanwhile, the Pakistani commander also ordered his troops to load their weapons, to create more fear in Ashok.

By this time, Ashok was standing at the main entrance with a young enemy soldier nudging him beneath his right rib cage with the cold steel of his rifle's bayonet. Ashok felt a chill run down his spine but continued standing there, undaunted. The young soldier's hands were trembling and his finger on the trigger was jittery, which was an unmistakable reminder of Ashok's precarious position.

To make matters worse, it was clear that the panicky soldier had never been in such close proximity to his adversary, which only added to the threat because he could overreact without considering the consequences.

It was as if for a minute all the years in between had vanished and a young Ashok was once again standing in front of the wolf. Jolted by the teaching of his experience all those years ago, Ashok gathered all his wits and continued to persuade the Pakistani soldier with whom he was conversing. Meanwhile, he turned to look at the young soldier holding the rifle to him, right in the eye and it was in that moment when he realized that once again he was in front of the lone wolf. Without breaking eye contact, Ashok went on to, quietly but confidently, put his hand on the barrel and slowly push it away from his body.

The soldier too silently relented. He had every reason to believe that in this game of psychological warfare, Ashok was now in the lead. With that conviction, Ashok realized that the enemy was almost swayed with his narrative and now it was time to play the final card in the emotional salvo.

Ashok now single-mindedly engaged in inflicting reminders of their families back home on the soldiers. He also assured them a safe passage back to their units, as opposed to a certain torturous death they would otherwise be destined to face should they fall into the hands of the Mukti Bahini, who would not settle for anything less than revenge on the people who held the family of their beloved Bangabandhu hostage.

The last card was his ace of spades as it brought about the realization of their dire situation, resulting in their yielding eventually. Instantly, Ashok rushed into the house and pushed open the doors to secure the family and mitigate any chances of foul play. He had indeed won this battle of guts and wits as some would call it later, all by himself.

Mrs Sheikh Mujibur Rahman, almost unbelieving of the fact that they had really been freed from their ordeal, embraced Ashok at once, saying, 'God Himself has sent you to save us . . . You are like my son!' Ashok smiled as he looked around and saw the immense sense of relief wash over the faces of the rest of the members of Mujib's family, which included his daughters Sheikh Hasina, Sheikh Rehana and son, Sheikh Russel.

Closing his eyes, Ashok finally allowed himself to breathe and took a moment to think of his own family, of his young wife and unborn baby back home and thanked God for letting his plan triumph.

9

A Perseverant Victory

As the surrendered men of the Pakistan Army were being taken away to the headquarters, they were questioned by the ever-curious media about what made them put their arms down. The commander of the contingent unflinchingly told them about the *bekhauf* (fearless) Indian Army officer, who had compelled them to surrender. Making good on his promise of providing safe passage to their destination, Ashok made them change out of their uniforms before sending them with his men to their headquarters. Their uniforms could have made them a target of the now victorious, but still angry, Mukti Bahini and he didn't want them to get harmed on their way.

As soon as the house was cleared of the enemy and the family of the Bangabandhu had been secured, the Bangabandhu's cousin, Khoka, who had also been held hostage (albeit at a different place and had been released a day prior), came forward with the flag of their country, Bangladesh, and urged Ashok to do the honours and replace the Pakistani flag on the roof with this. Ashok respectfully obliged and as soon as he unfurled the flag of their now-liberated nation, it was followed by loud cries of 'Joi Bangla!' by the family and onlookers alike. For everyone standing there, it was truly a moment of triumph! Ashok was even told by Khoka that he was the first person to have hoisted the national flag of Bangladesh on top of the Bangabandhu's house after the liberation of Bangladesh.

Later on, the same day (17 December 1971) at 8 p.m., Mrs Gandhi declared:

> . . . India has no territorial ambitions. Now that Pakistani armed forces have surrendered in Bangladesh and Bangladesh is free, it is pointless in our view to continue the present conflict.[1]

The *New York Times* article by Charles Mohr, published on 17 December 1971, amongst other details of the surrender, also mentioned the fate of Sheikh Mujibur Rahman. It read:

> One of the most important of those matters is the fate of Sheik Mujibur Rahman, the charismatic East Bengali politician who is under arrest in West Pakistan for treason.

> India will exert as much pressure as possible on General Yahya to release Sheik Mujib—as he is popularly known—who has been proclaimed president by the Bengali secessionists. who call their territory Bangladesh (Bengal Nation). Indian officials fear that if he is not released chaos and a struggle for power may boil over in East Pakistan.[2]

Soon after, Ashok's unit, 14 Guards, which had been deployed at the airport, was detailed to move back out of Dhaka to Mizoram. Now that the war had been won and Bangladesh had been liberated, the Indian Army's job was done and they had to fall back to their original locations and get back to performing their usual tasks. As Charles Mohr wrote at the end of his report:

> The Bengalis are said to have agreed that initial steps to restore law and order, public amenities and utilities would be carried out by the 'unified command' of Indian and Bangladesh soldiers, in which the Indians are senior.
>
> 'But believe me,' said an Indian official of high rank privately, 'we want to get out of Bangladesh as soon as possible. We do not want to become or even seem to appear to be an occupying force.'[3]

However, Ashok was asked to stay back. As soon as word reached Sheikh Mujibur Rahman, who had been under arrest in Pakistan, about his family's plight and the heroic rescue by a young Ashok, he expressed a strong desire to meet the brave officer and requested for him to be held back until his return. Since it was a goodwill gesture by none other than the leader of Bangladesh, the officials on the Indian side understood and therefore Ashok was asked to stay behind.

Ashok was not only surprised but also deeply touched by this gesture. As a thoroughbred army officer, Ashok felt that he had only been performing his duty, but to be acknowledged for it in this manner warmed his heart.

Since the Bangabandhu's return was still some time away, his family and colleagues took it upon themselves to ensure that Ashok's stay was comfortable and he wasn't left wanting for anything. Not only was he put up in comfortable accommodation, he was also given a personal car that remained with him at all times for him to be able to travel around conveniently. As the city wasn't familiar to him, more often than not, Sheikh Jamal, the younger son of Sheikh Mujibur Rahman, would accompany him and play tour guide.

As the Bangabandhu and his family were greatly loved and revered by the people of Bangladesh, the story of their rescue had travelled to the rest of the city in no time and within a few days, almost everybody knew the story of the valiant Indian Army officer, who had fearlessly gone in unarmed and rescued their beloved leader's family.

As a result, in the days following the rescue, Ashok would always be received with deep respect and admiration by the locals. No matter where he went, his story seemed to precede him and earn him the love of the people even before he had a chance to be in front of them physically. The appreciation ran so deep that even when he stepped out into the market to make purchases, however big or small, the shopkeepers would absolutely refuse to accept any payment from him, despite his protests. In fact, after a few days of the rescue, the acting prime minister of Bangladesh, Tajuddin Ahmad, was received by Maj. Ashok Tara as per army norms.

One day, Sheikh Jamal, the younger son of Sheikh Mujibur Rahman, invited him out for lunch at a roadside restaurant. It was a welcome break for Ashok and he looked forward to having an authentic Bangladeshi meal out, which he thoroughly enjoyed. As soon as they had finished their food and asked for the bill, the young owner not only declined to take any money, he, in fact, placed a ten-rupee note in front of Ashok and asked him to autograph it for him as a souvenir. He said that Ashok was responsible for the safe lives of the first family of Bangladesh and its citizens had to make sure to treat him in the manner that, according to them, he truly deserved. He was their hero.

It's a completely surreal experience to explore a country after a bloody war has ended. News of the rescue must have travelled far and wide, but Ashok took it all in his stride. He was visibly moved by the warmth of the Bangladeshi people of course, but he was constantly aware that this was his job. He would have gone about his assignment with the same determination irrespective of who had been held hostage in that house. The fact that it was Mujibur's family only made the act all the more important to Bangladesh's victory.

Meanwhile, Ashok would also visit the family of the Sheikh regularly. Bangamata, as Sheikh Mujibur Rahman's wife fondly came to be known in the days following the rescue, grew very fond of Ashok and treated him with the same warmth and affection as she did her sons. She even addressed him as *beta* (son) while conversing. The children, on the other hand, also became friendly with him in due course. Sheikh Rehana, Mujib's younger daughter, would address him as *dada* or elder brother, and even went on to write letters to him after he left Dhaka. Ashok had become family to these people now and there were no restrictions on his visits to their house. In fact, one day, Mrs Rahman presented him with a brand new Tissot watch and insisted that he accept it as a token of her affection. Unable to argue with the elderly lady, Ashok humbly accepted the gift.

While life was returning to normal post-war in the new country of Bangladesh, their elected leader, Sheikh Mujibur Rahman, was still far away from them, in the custody of the Government of Pakistan which, by this time, was being governed by Zulfikar Ali Bhutto. After the surrender of the West Pakistani forces to the Indian forces, the entire blame for the breakdown of the country of Pakistan, along with its defeat in the war, had been laid unforgivingly at Gen. Yahya Khan's door, who resigned from the command of the military on 20 December 1971 and handed over the reins of the leadership of the county to Zulfikar Ali Bhutto.

According to a *New York Times* article, published on 18 January 1972, Bhutto had met the Bangabandhu soon after taking over command. Giving some details of their interaction, it stated:

> After a few days, Mr. Bhutto, the leader of the majority party in the West, who had collaborated with the army in the moves that led to the crackdown and repression in East Pakistan, went to see Sheik Mujib, who said he greeted him: 'Bhutto, what are you doing here?' Sheik Mujib says he had learned of Mr. Bhutto's accession to power but was doing a little leg pulling.
>
> 'I am the President and also the chief martial-law administrator,' was the reply, according to Sheik Mujib. 'A wonderful situation.'
>
> Mr. Bhutto said, Sheik Mujib recalled, that when General Yahya Khan was handing over power to him, he said that his one great regret was that he had not killed Sheik Mujib and asked if he could 'finish this one piece of work.' Mr. Bhutto told Sheik Mujib that the general offered to predate the papers so it would appear that the execution took place under him. Mr. Bhutto refused.

Sheik Mujib said today that the reason he refused was largely political. Mr. Bhutto reasoned, he said, that if the Bengali leader was executed, they would kill the nearly 100, 000 Pakistani soldiers who had surrendered in East Pakistan and then the people of the Punjab and the North-West Frontier Province—where most of the West Pakistani troops come from—would blame Mr. Bhutto and rise against his Government.

Sheik Mujib said that Mr. Bhutto kept pressing him to enter into negotiations to retain some link, no matter how tenuous, between the two Pakistani regions.

'I told him I had to know one thing first—am I free or not?' Sheik Mujib said. 'If I'm free, let me go. If I'm not, I cannot talk.'

'You're free,' he quoted Mr. Bhutto as saying, 'but I need a few days before I can let you go.'

Despite the promise of freedom, Sheik Mujib said, he did not discuss substantive matters with Mr. Bhutto.

At another point, when Mr. Bhutto had been contending that the two wings were still united by law and tradition, Sheik Mujib—reminding him that the Awami League won a national majority in the last election, the results of which were never honoured — said: 'Well, if Pakistan is still one country, then you are not President and chief martial-law administrator. I am.'

> On Jan. 7 the President went to see Sheik Mujib for the third and last time. The Bengali leader said he told him: 'You must free me tonight. There is no more room for delay. Either free me or kill me.'
>
> Sheik Mujib said Mr. Bhutto replied that it was difficult to make arrangements at such short notice, but finally agreed to fly him to London. Sheik Mujib said that as Mr. Bhutto saw him off, he was still asking him to consider a political tie with West Pakistan.[4]

While on the other hand Britain's *Sunday Telegraph* carried a quote from Bhutto stating:

> I plan to release him (Sheikh Mujib) unconditionally in a couple of days, with hope and faith that the fire of Pakistan still burns in his heart. He will be free to go. I am not extracting any promise from him . . . From one end of the spectrum to the other, an extremely loose arrangement could be worked out, but at least the name of Pakistan must remain. It's our legacy of 1,000 years and we can't spurn it.

Although he was also quoted by the *Daily Telegraph* where he said:

> One thing is clear, however. Mujib is not going to be influenced by me or anyone else. His mind is his own.

The Bangabandhu, after bidding farewell to Bhutto was finally flown in a special PIA aircraft on 8 January 1972, from Chaklala airport in Rawalpindi, followed by Bhutto telling the media that:

> The nightingale has flown.

As soon as he arrived in London, Sheikh Mujibur Rahman was driven to central London, to the Claridges hotel. One of the first people to meet the Bangabandhu in the hotel was Britain's opposition leader, Harold Wilson, who greeted him warmly with the words, 'Good morning Mr President,' words so simple and apt but that had come at a dear cost to the new leader of the country of Bangladesh.

Sheikh Mujibur Rahman, thin and frail-looking owing to his days of imprisonment, then had to address a crowded press conference at the hotel on the afternoon of 8 January 1972. His opening remarks were:

> Today I am free to share the unbounded joy of freedom with my fellow countrymen, who have won their freedom in an epic liberation struggle.
>
> The ultimate achievement of this struggle is the creation of an independent, sovereign. People's Republic of Bangladesh, of which my people declared me as their president while I was a prisoner in the condemned cell, awaiting the execution of a sentence for hanging.[5]

Finally, on 10 January 1972, Sheikh Mujibur Rahman, after breaking his journey to meet with the Indian president and prime minister at Delhi airport, took off for his home, his free country of which he was going to be the first president. As he landed at the Dhaka airport, a massive crowd of people surged towards it, holding life-sized posters of their beloved Bangabandhu. The people of Bangladesh had suffered but had fought back untiringly for almost ten long months and were finally going to be reunited with the one man who had not only led them, but had also instilled confidence in them to fight back. He had encouraged them to rise to the occasion and claim their rights. Their liberator was coming back to them, alive and well. Their trials and tribulations were finally being replaced with joy and jubilation and the atmosphere was of long-awaited happiness. As the citizens of Bangladesh moved together to welcome their leader back, their minds were relieved, their hearts were full and their mouths couldn't stop cheering their victory as they relentlessly shouted 'Joi Bangla! Joi Bangabandhu!' interspersed with the occasional patriotic songs that they kept breaking into. The voices of the people were loud enough to muffle the twenty-one-gun salute that an artillery regiment had carried out to mark the homecoming of their leader.

It was a day of well-deserved celebration and as someone who had played a big part in bringing it about, Ashok looked on, carrying much of the happiness that the citizens of the country were feeling in his own heart.

No sooner had the Sheikh returned, when Ashok received an official invite to breakfast with him on the morning of 12 January 1972. As an excited, albeit nervous, Ashok stood in front of the much loved and talked about Bangabandhu, he realized that his nervousness was unfounded. For Mujib had nothing but immense gratitude in his heart as well as many kind words for the saviour of his family. He too, within a few minutes of meeting Ashok, declared that he was like his son, a man sent by God Himself, to save his family from the jaws of a certain death!

During the course of their conversation, Ashok couldn't help but feel for the powerful but emotional man in front of him. Although his country had been liberated and his family was now safe, his pain from the suffering of his own people and the inhumane treatment meted out to them by the enemy was still raw. Ashok realized that their victory had come at a debilitating cost and Mujib was not going to get over it any time soon. As a humble and gracious Mujib spoke to him, Ashok couldn't miss the heaviness of heart with which he spoke about healing the wounds of his people. He had to restore their dignity and pride along with their economy and the weight of the task at hand was immense. Ashok realised that this milestone victory came at a heavy price paid in the form of human lives. Every celebration was tinged with sadness at the recent bloodshed. With a heavy but content heart, Ashok finally took his leave and returned home.

He left for Delhi on 23 January 1972. However, before he left, he met with the family again for lunch on 22 January 1972. At his last meeting with the family before leaving, Sheikh Hasina presented him with a picture of herself with her three-month-old son, Joi, with a note at the back that said, 'with best wishes to Abha bhabi, from Hasina and Joi, 22.1.72,' as a souvenir for his wife, Abha. Finally, Ashok was dropped off at the airport by a member of the first family, Khoka, with whom he had become good friends during the course of his time in the country, who gave him a bouquet of flowers before bidding him a fond farewell. Ashok was sent to Calcutta from Dhaka in an air force flight and he was to travel back to his family in Delhi by train.

On his way home, Ashok wondered whether his family was even aware of what he had been doing and all that he had been a part of until the end of the war. There had been no communication with them in all this time, so he was unaware of their understanding of the situation. When he arrived at his doorstep, surprising everyone, including his wife and baby, the family was thrilled. To his surprise, he was told how they had been asked by their neighbour to watch the news on 17 December 1971, as Ashok's act of valour was being featured. As they had switched the TV on, Abha had walked into the room from the kitchen to stand quietly in a corner, watching the news about her husband from whom she had been separated for several months. The family beamed with pride and joy at seeing his name on the TV even though they did not fully understand the significance of his actions yet. With their little baby in tow, Abha had maintained a calm demeanour while he had been away, for the sake of the family, even though her thoughts would wander sometimes and she would worry about his safety. It was time for her, just like the rest of the household, to heave a sigh of relief and look forward to spending time with Ashok.

Ashok had returned home with his own stories of the war . . . this time for his father and the generations to come.

10

The Aftermath

After a well-deserved and much-needed break, which included spending time with his new-born daughter Anshu, Ashok joined his unit back in Mizoram. The year had started on a high and busy note for him, so he welcomed the return to the routine in the months following that.

Soon, 14 Guards finished their tenure in Mizoram and geared up to move to a new location. This time it was to move to a peace station, which happened to be Kanpur in Uttar Pradesh. Thus, by the end of August 1972, they moved to Kanpur and conducted their training in Almorah, Uttar Pradesh.

Although Kanpur was a peace station, the unit was destined to see action here as well.

In 1973, the Uttar Pradesh Provincial Armed Constabulary (PAC) which is a state armed-police force, saw its people revolting. The units are maintained at key locations across the state and activated only upon explicit orders from the deputy inspector general and other higher authorities. They were established to deal with serious law-and-order situations along with calamities. They were also assigned VIP duties during festivities, elections, natural disasters, communal riots, etc. They exist in addition to the normal police force and are equipped with semi-automatic rifles as well as *lathis* (bamboo sticks) for mob control during unrest.

The 1973 revolt was a mutiny by three battalions of PAC, located at Bareilly, Meerut and Agra. Their issues were:

a. Deep discontent about meagre wages.
b. Resentment about being made to do menial jobs like doing the laundry or the dishes for other senior officials.
c. No residential quarters, mess or vehicles despite long hours of work.
d. Not allowed to make an association or union.

Even though the battalions involved in the revolt were located in different cities, it was Lucknow that became ground zero for it. On 23 May 1973, all examinations of Lucknow University were called off and a few incidents of arson were reported. The revolt was started by the PAC unit deployed on the campus of the university but was also joined by the students of the university.

The *New York Times* also carried an article reporting on the matter, in its issue dated 23 May 1973. It said:

> Indian troops battled a state police force in Uttar Pradesh today in an attempt to put down a rebellion among the policemen.
>
> Informed sources here said at least 30 persons were killed and many wounded in heavy exchange of fire between the army and the Provincial Armed Constabulary, a paramilitary reserve force kept by the state government to aid the regular police.
>
> Official sources here said that there were 18,000 to 20,000 constabulary men in Uttar Pradesh and that most of them had been disarmed. However, several groups were reported holding out.
>
> The flare-up has shaken both New Delhi and the state government. Officials fear the discontent may spread to the regular police, as well as to police units in other states.
>
> Uttar Pradesh, in northern India, is especially vulnerable because of the security problem posed by the presence of a large number of Pakistani prisoners of war at camps there.

According to reports from Lucknow, the state capital, some men of the Armed Constabulary joined with student arsonists yesterday in burning part of the city's ancient university.

The constabulary was posted on the campus at the request of teachers supervising an examination, who feared the student violence that often erupts at examination time. In past years students protesting stiff examinations or admonitions against cheating have assaulted teachers.

Members of the constabulary known to resent their poor pay and service conditions, have been agitating for improvements.

On Sunday night student leaders and officials of the constabulary were said to have conferred and decided on a joint protest. A midnight procession was organized in which slogans hailed the fraternity of the students and police.

The university authorities asked the Government to replace the constabulary with troops, but there was a three hour delay before the military moved in. During this time students and some constabulary men reportedly went on a rampage, setting fire to several buildings and breaking furniture. According to reports from the area, a large part of the university was ablaze yesterday.

State Order Resisted

A state government order to disarm the police was resisted by members of the constabulary at Kanpur and Ramnagar near Benares, where the largest barracks are situated. Heavy exchanges of fire were reported as well as minor clashes in four other towns.

New Delhi officials said that the Uttar Pradesh government had ordered an inquiry into the incidents and that Lucknow University had been closed indefinitely.

The university, one of India's largest, has 6,000 students. Last week there was a minor arson attempt in one of its buildings.

University authorities say that the flare-up would have been avoided if the armed police had not been brought into the university. But the teachers refused to supervise the examinations until they were given protection.

Eventually, the army was summoned to quell the para-military forces in the state, while the wave reached the PAC unit located in Kanpur as well. On 24 May 1973, Ashok was ordered to move with the Alpha company of 14 Guards to the Kanpur PAC lines/unit to suppress the revolt. There was information that some of the officers and their families were held in the custody of the PAC men and so, one of the tasks assigned to Ashok was to rescue them.

Once again, Ashok found himself responsible for the lives and safety of innocent people, but this time, he was armed with the experience of one of the most daring rescue operations anyone had ever done.

To hide their identity, Ashok decided to move with a small reconnaissance (recce) group in mufti towards the PAC lines/unit in Kanpur. Despite their painstaking efforts to go incognito, the other side came to know of their plan, stopping and surrounding them at the exit gate of the unit. As soon as they were exposed, the men of the PAC separated Ashok from his group and held him under house arrest in one of the guest houses on the campus.

At the guest house, Ashok discovered that the family of a senior police official was being held hostage. This family included a child. Although he had previously been a part of a rescue operation, this time, he himself was one of the hostages. He steeled himself to the task at hand and decided to only think about making sure that the family was rescued safely. He had to deal with the situation with single-minded focus.

Time was of the essence, so he dived into thinking up a feasible plan to carry out the rescue. Taking a leaf out of his experience in Bangladesh, he started talking sympathetically to the sentry who was on guard duty at their gate. Trying to engage the enemy psychologically had worked for him earlier as well, so he was confident of his skill with this approach. Fortunately for him, no sooner had he started the conversation than he sensed that he was gaining the confidence of the guard. When he had first been brought in, the guard had been zealously restricting the prisoners' movements to the bare minimum. However, as soon as he started chatting with Ashok, answering his questions and volunteering useful titbits of information on his own, Ashok used the opportunity to take small liberties, just a few steps here and there to ostensibly stretch his legs a little. He established that the guard was indeed loosening control and lowering his guard as he was suitably distracted with the conversation that Ashok had initiated.

Ashok understood the sensitivity of the situation. They had to move fast in order to push home their advantage, but they couldn't afford to make any mistakes by jumping the gun. Therefore, he waited patiently for an opportunity to carry out the plan he had in mind. He got his window to move a little away when the guard started to doze off. Acting swiftly, Ashok opened the back door and helped the family, including the child, escape. This was done in the wee hours, around 4 a.m. on 25 May 1973. The family moved out quickly, but not without turning back to smile gratefully at their rescuer. Ashok heaved a sigh of relief and smiled back at them.

On 24 May 1973, the *New York Times* published another article about the revolt as a follow up to the one published the previous day. It said:

A police rebellion that has taken 40 lives since it began yesterday here in Uttar Pradesh continued for the second day today in three towns.

Police officials in this state capital reported that insurgent members of the 20,000-man paramilitary reserve force known as the Provincial Armed Constabulary were defying army orders to lay down their weapons in Jehamgirabad, Gorakhpur and Ghurma.

Since the revolt began, 600 men have been reported arrested and many others disarmed and confined to barracks. Officials said that 13 soldiers, 25 policemen and two civilians had died in the fighting that had followed an army move at dawn yesterday to disarm all dissidents.

Constabulary members, or state policemen, agitating for higher pay, better service conditions and the right to organize a trade union, joined student demonstrators at Lucknow University on Monday in a wave of rioting and arson. Troops called in to quell the police rebellion exchanged fire with dissidents yesterday in at least half a dozen places

Today the army was ordered to avoid opening fire as far as possible in its efforts to disarm the holdouts.

At Jehangirabad, 25 miles from here, 300 insurgents were reported under siege. The rebels were said to have shut themselves inside an ancient fort with at least 17 of their officers as hostages.

While resistance also continued at Gorakhpur and Ghurma, constabulary members at Fatehpur surrendered after having controlled two armouries there for 24 hours.

In the meantime, as soon as word reached Ashok's unit, they sent reinforcements to help their officer and his men, who were reported to be under house arrest. They reached the campus and quickly got deployed around the area, encircling the place where Ashok and his men were held. The next step was to issue a warning to the men of the PAC to release their officer and their troops amicably to avoid conflict. But as their word of caution went unheeded, the only option left was to begin firing.

As soon as the army troops started firing, the PAC retaliated with fire from their end. Firing from the Indian Army's side is not something that could ever be taken lightly and it created quite a furore amongst the PAC. Quick to sense their panic from inside his prison and taking advantage of the confusion before the sentry guarding him could realize it, Ashok made a dash towards his own troops. Thus, even though the few PAC who saw his getaway tried to deter him by shooting at him, he kept running under fire and made a beeline to his destination, managing to eventually jump over the wire fence and reunite with his men. Ashok had escaped custody and joined his own troops in what seemed like the blink of an eye.

The rescue of the police official's family, along with Ashok's escape, even under fire, shook the confidence of the men of the PAC to counter the troops of the army. As desired, the PAC insurgents surrendered within the next few hours, resulting in the effective suppression of the revolt.

However, since the unrest had managed to gain nationwide attention, it resulted in the resignation of the Congress ministry, headed by Kamalapati Tripathi, and president's rule was imposed.

Fortunately for Ashok, the period following this incident was calm and he could enjoy some peace, harmony and family time with his wife and baby girl, Anshu, and could also be around for the birth of his second child in Kanpur on 12 December 1973, a son whom the parents lovingly named Ashish.

Thereafter, Ashok went on to have a fruitful and satisfying career in the army, serving in places like Poonch, Karnataka (where he commanded a unit of the NCC), Pune, Mizoram and Arunachal Pradesh. While he enjoyed training the young cadets of the NCC, he also continued to be involved in operations, many a time taking crucial decisions that would tip the balance in favour of the side he was on. He never forgot the lessons that he had learnt through his experiences in the liberation war and made sure to use them at every opportunity he got.

After serving as the second-in-command for sometime, by the year 1984, Ashok subsequently took over the command of the unit, 14 Guards, as a colonel at Nasirabad (Rajasthan) with an operational role in Jaisalmer. As the commanding officer, Ashok made sure to always keep the welfare of his officers and men at the forefront of his thoughts while passing the fruits of his experience down to them, to groom and prepare them to always be able to perform their duties to the best of their abilities and unflinchingly, even in the face of adversities, just as he had. In operational matters, his priority would always be the safety of his troops, even if it meant flying in the face of official orders at times. However, his experience never let him down and his decisions were always impeccable. After their peace tenure in Rajasthan, the unit eventually moved to Poonch in Jammu and Kashmir, which was a field station, in 1986.

After his tenure as commanding officer in Rajouri-Poonch, Jammu and Kashmir, again one of the active areas, in the year 1988, Ashok was posted to the beautiful hills of Yol in Dharamshala at the Station Headquarters.

Interestingly, the word 'Yol' was coined by the British guards. It is where the Italian POWs were held during World War II. These POWs did not understand the English language very well, therefore, whenever they had to be recalled to their lines (the place where they stayed) from their prisoners' camp, the word YOL, which stood for 'your own lines/location', was used. It simply meant that they had to return to their location and eventually, the location came to be known as Yol.

After enjoying the scenic beauty of the calm and peaceful hills of Yol, life came a full circle when Ashok was posted to Delhi, his hometown where he served in the Army Headquarters till July 1992.

In the end he got posted to Sukna, which is located in the foothills of Darjeeling in Headquarter 33 Corps. From here he travelled to various forward units in places like Darjeeling, Sikkim and even the Indo-China border, including the Nathula Pass, eventually retiring after finishing his tenure, from Sukna.

Colonel Ashok Tara, after serving an illustrious and enviable career in the Indian Army, finally hung up his uniform on 31 January 1994.

Epilogue

The Lone Wolf Now

Time is unpredictable, and according to the proverb, 'Time and tide wait for no man.' Life is meant to move with the times, to ride the ebb and flow of tides. It's all a state of mind whether one smiles or broods over one's lot in life, be it professional, social or personal.

After the hospitality and honour conferred by Sheikh Mujibur Rahman's family (including the current Prime Minister Sheikh Hasina), as well as the locals of Dhaka and Mr Shamin Ahmed, CEO of Nautundhara Foundation (author and publishers), I left Dhaka on 23 January 1972.

From the airport in Dhaka I took off on an Indian Air Force plane for Calcutta and then onward on my own to my hometown, Delhi. My unit, 14 Guards, sanctioned my sixty-day annual leave. I joyously spent my long-overdue vacation with my family, especially with Abha, my wife, and my new-born daughter, Anshu.

After my leave, I re-joined my unit at Mizoram. By then I had received two letters from Sheikh Rehana, the younger daughter of Sheikh Mujibur Rahman (who addressed me as Dada/Bhaiya) to convey her gratitude for saving their family from captivity. It was a touching gesture, one that I cherish till date. I immediately replied to her, but she never received my letters. This was probably because of security reasons as I was still in active service in the army, and/or because of political reasons. Except for this, there was no further communication between me and the first family of Bangladesh. The only information I got was through the media.

In the years following that, during my service in the army, the rescue of the family of Sheikh Mujibur Rahman was downplayed as an insignificant action and not given any publicity—perhaps because I did not have a powerful godfather rooting for me. Another possible reason could have been that every individual involved in the war, from the commanders of the units and others in the higher echelons, were too busy garnering credit for themselves in the great victory that the liberation war of Bangladesh had turned out to be in December 1971, to acknowledge comparatively small fry like me. While a number of events and people were appreciated in the history of the war, the rescue of the first family was set aside without being given its due credit until the Hon'ble Prime Minister Sheikh Hasina of Bangladesh brought it into the limelight because of its significance and impact on the history of Bangladesh.

20 October 2012: Day of Glory

After my retirement in the year 1994, I was redeployed in the army for a period of six months. Subsequently, I dabbled in a couple of things professionally, before realizing that the civilian way of working and ethics did not conform to my values.

Finally, upon the advice of some senior veterans, I started a real estate office to help veterans and serving army men deal with sales/purchase of property, as most of them were naive in such dealings. The business turned out well and I am comfortably running the same till date. My bitter experiences also made me gravitate towards social service and other welfare associations, especially those that were linked to veterans and their families. My children, Anshu (daughter) and Ashish (son) settled in Melbourne, Australia, with their families including Sanyogita (my daughter-in-law) and Rhea (granddaughter) while I chose to remain in Noida with my wife, Abha, staying close to our friends as I started a new chapter in my life.

Life was going on normally when, early one morning, towards the end of September 2012, I received a telephone call from my friend and neighbour, Col Bal. He asked me to switch on the transistor to hear the news. The Bangladesh government formally announced on air their intention to confer an award called 'Friends of Bangladesh Liberation War Honour' to Col Ashok Tara. Me. It was as if all the years in between had disappeared and I was back in Bangladesh, in my beloved uniform, enthusiastically carrying out all the tasks I had been assigned. The house, the young guard with his bayonet lodged on my lower ribs, the voice of Bangamata calling out a warning to me from within, all of it flashed before my eyes. Had it really been over forty years ago? It was hard to comprehend the passage of time, and hearing that radio announcement unlocked memories that had been stored away for decades. It was very much like dusting an old room, letting the sunshine in, and finding artefacts from a time far, far away in the past.

A lot had changed in all our lives as well. Aside from Sheikh Hasina, the prime minister, and Sheikh Rehana, her younger sister, Sheikh Mujibur Rehman and his entire family had been assassinated on 15 August 1975. It is a different kind of grief that I experienced when I learnt of the brutal assassination. Strong emotions came bubbling to the surface at the unfortunate fate of the family that I had given my all to save, just a few years before that ghastly act.

As it turned out, Abha and I were invited to Dhaka, Bangladesh on 18 October 2012 for the award ceremony. Upon hearing the news, Abha turned to me with an affectionate and understanding smile; as always, my strong and ever-supportive wife, who had stood by me through thick and thin. Although it had been delayed by several decades, my recognition had finally come. I was overjoyed. I was pleased that I didn't go chasing any recognition to begin with; I had always viewed the rescue as something that had to be done in the line of duty. But I would be lying if I said that it didn't fill me with immense pride to have been conferred with this award.

The next few days passed in a whirl of preparation for our trip and after all of forty-one years, I finally set foot in the land that had given me my most valuable lessons of life. This time with my life partner in tow, which multiplied my joy. On 20 October 2012, I was conferred the award, 'Friends of Liberation War Honour', by Prime Minister Sheikh Hasina along with Mr Nazrul Islam, acting president of Bangladesh. I was meeting her after more than forty years. It was one of the most glorious days of my life second only to the time when the gallantry award, the Vir Chakra, was bestowed on me by V.V. Giri, the president of India, on 24 November 1972 at the Rashtrapati Bhavan, New Delhi.

While in Bangladesh, I also had the good fortune of meeting the wife of the PVC awardee of my unit, the 14 Guards, L/Nk Albert Ekka. Albert and I had fought side by side and had been awarded gallantry awards for the battle of Gangasagar. While I had lived to tell the tale, my brother-in-arms had sacrificed his life, courageously and in the highest traditions of the Indian Army. To be revisiting the land where we had fought side by side, with his bereaved family representing him, was an indescribably moving experience.

The award ceremony was telecast live on Bangladesh TV and was covered well by the media in both countries (India and Bangladesh). Abha and I were also invited by the hon'ble prime minister to her residence, where she shared her memories of the rescue with my wife. Listening to her, I realized just how clearly the memory of that fateful day had been etched in her mind, just as it was etched in mine. The thought humbled me.

After my return from Dhaka, my family, who had watched the telecast, came over to tell me how happy and proud they were of me. Jubilant friends and neighbours received us with garlands and bouquets, and they had also arranged a small reception party. I was truly overwhelmed.

I often felt that after years of living in a certain kind of anonymity, this award placed me on the path of glory and pride as a soldier of the great Indian Army. I felt that an act in the line of my duty was at long last being honoured by both the army and civilian population.

From then onwards, I was bestowed with many honours in various forums at district, state, national and international levels. A few of them are:

NGOs

a. Umeed Hai at Noida (UP) conferred: 'Pride of Noida' on 22 December 2013.
b. Spiritual Life Foundation-Parmarsh bestowed 'Pride of Gautum Budh Nagar' on Vijay Diwas, 14 August 2019.
c. Local organizations at both state and district levels invited and honoured me on various occasions.

Veterans Organizations

(a) Veterans India Foundation (all over India), New Delhi, honoured me by presenting me with 'Veteran of the Year 2017' award by the minister and ex-army chief Gen. V.K. Singh at the NCC auditorium, Delhi Cantonment.
(b) Fauji Group Organization, Pune, Maharashtra, invited me to give a talk to veterans, their families and the local media about the 1971 war, especially the battle of Gangasagar, for which I was awarded the Vir Chakra

and on the rescue of the then first family of Bangladesh. It was published with my photo in the newspapers of Pune.

(c) Shaheed Samark, Noida, UP. During Victory Day 2018 the committee invited me to speak to the Indian Army veterans and a few others about the battle of Gangasagar and the rescue of the family of Hon'ble Sheikh Hasina of Bangladesh. This was planned after the official visit of Sheikh Hasina to Honour the Martyrs of Liberation War of 1971 at Manekshaw Hall, Delhi Cantonment. It was published in the national and state local papers. The Shaheed Samark, Noida, also published an article in their annual magazine.

Educational Institutes

(a) Puduchery. Talk on the battle of Gangasagar and rescue of the family of Hon'ble PM Sheikh Hasina to the students of educational institutes.
    (i) 'VIRAJA TRUST' by Shyam Kumari, publisher and distributors of Aurobindo Ashram, Puduchery.
    (ii) Girls' College of Puduchery.

(b) K.R. Mangalam World School, Vaishali, Ghaziabad, UP, invited me on 16 August 2019 to give a motivational talk to the students about the 1971 war and the rescue of the family of Bangabandhu, Bangladesh. They honoured me by presenting a statue of Saraswati.

(c) Jawaharlal Nehru University (JNU), New Delhi.

(i) Invited by the Veterans India Association with the Alumni Association of JNU to inaugurate 'THE WALL OF HEROES' along with the vice chancellor, Jagadesh Kumar, at the Conventional Hall, JNU. This wall displays photos of twenty-one Param Vir Chakra awardees.

(ii) Once again, on 6 December 2018, I was invited to JNU to commemorate the Bangladesh Liberation War 1971.

Now that our children have settled in Melbourne, Australia, my wife and I have been visiting them regularly. In 2015, during one of these visits, the Army Veteran Group and the Consulate of the Indian High Commission came to know of my presence there. They were excited and invited Abha and me to join them for the Australia-New Zealand Army Corps (ANZAC), including Indian troops, Day Parade, a national day at Melbourne. They wanted to honour me for my role in the rescue of Sheikh Mujibur Rahman's family and for having been conferred the award, 'Friends of Liberation War Honour', by the Bangladesh Government. The ANZAC Parade is celebrated as a National Day to honour the martyrs who, on 25 April 1915, landed at Gallipoli, Turkey, during World War I.

Later, a local magazine in Melbourne, the *Indian Weekly*, published an issue with my photo on its cover with the caption, 'Hero Soldier', and mentioned my rescue of Bangladesh's first family in 1971. Another magazine, *G Days India*, published an article titled, 'He Gambled with Life to Save the First Family of Bangladesh'. It was gratifying.

Now, whenever I visit Melbourne, I'm always invited to participate in the ANZAC Parade and other such social functions.

Needless to say, the recognition and appreciation that I had craved for years had started pouring in, even if a little late, but I had no complaints. I did not expect anything more. God has been kind.

Little did I know that destiny had other plans.

It was just another summer morning in April 2017, in my house in Noida. I was going about my daily routine when the phone rang. The number was unknown, so I braced myself for an unsolicited conversation possibly with some call-centre employee. I couldn't have been more wrong. The call was from Army Headquarters in Delhi and after confirming my identity, the caller informed me about the impending arrival of the prime minister of Bangladesh for the 'Sommanona ceremony', during which she wanted to honour the officers and soldiers of the Indian Army who had been involved in the war of 1971, along with the martyrs. It was to be held on 8 April 2017, at the Manekshaw Centre in Delhi Cantonment. After providing the rest of the information about the ceremony and taking down details about my vehicle, etc., for security reasons, I was asked if I had any questions.

I had only one. 'Can I bring my wife?'

A little while later, the person called back to confirm that I could.

As I got ready for the function on the morning of 8 April 2017, I couldn't help but feel anxious about what the day held in store for me. The ceremony was to be attended by the prime minister of India, Narendra Modi. Over the last couple of years, I had been blessed to receive a lot of love and appreciation in both my own country and foreign lands, including Bangladesh and even Australia. But, to be honoured in my own homeland and at this overwhelming scale was mind-blowing. I donned my favourite brown suit, pinned my medals proudly on the left side of my chest, held the hand of my wonderful wife who looked as charming as ever in her pretty white-and-blue, floral-print saree, and stepped out to welcome the prime minister of Bangladesh, this time on Indian soil.

As our car pulled into the intimidating and impressively pillared portico of the Manekshaw Centre, just in time for the function, a JCO ran up to receive us. He confirmed our details as we alighted and then escorted us inside. Stepping into the massive auditorium, Abha and I quickly sat down in a couple of vacant seats in the seventh row, so as to not come in the way of the people buzzing around to welcome the chief guests. I had barely taken my seat, when I heard my friend call out from a distance, 'Ashok, the PM wants to meet you.'

Self-conscious about being the cynosure of all eyes, I made my way to the front row. I figured that being in the front would make it easier for us to exchange pleasantries with the prime minister of Bangladesh, Sheikh Hasina, if she so wished. However, after a few more minutes, Abha and I were ushered out to the foyer to be a part of the welcome party for Sheikh Hasina as soon as she arrived. Apparently, our honoured chief guest had specifically asked for this arrangement so that she could take a moment to have a comfortable conversation with me before the rest of the ceremony. This time we were escorted by the then chief of army staff (COAS), Gen. Bipin Rawat.

Abha and I, along with the COAS, stood waiting patiently in the foyer. Soon we saw Mrs Sheikh Hasina and Mr Narendra Modi descending the stairs in front of us. The prime ministers were chatting amicably as they slowly made their way towards the auditorium's entrance. Gen. Rawat stepped forward to greet them and called their attention to my wife and me. The prime minister of India greeted us with folded hands while I stood up tall and struck a salute in return. As soon as Mrs Sheikh Hasina saw me, she beamed at me and extended her hand to my wife who took it gently with a bow. Thereafter, she went on to excitedly narrate the story of the rescue to Mr Modi, who listened with a smile on his face, as she said, '*Humnein inko bola, nahin! Jana nahin, humein bacha ke jana. Koi aitbaar mat karna in par, julmi hain, kabhi hi goli chala denge or kisi ko mar denge* (We told him, no, don't leave, leave only after rescuing us! Don't trust them, they are brutal, they will shoot any time and kill anyone).'

Mr Modi said to me, '*Apko dekh kar ke to wo bohot khush hain* (She is so happy to see you).'

I would be lying if I said I could have imagined standing in front of two prime ministers while they discussed my achievements. Yet here I was, living that moment and soaking it all in.

As our cavalcade slowly moved in, with the photographers making a passageway for the two PMs, I bade adieu with another salute and then followed the procession into the auditorium to take my seat. Mrs Hasina walked alongside Mr Modi, admiring the pictures of the liberation war adorning the walls of the gallery. One of the photographs had a younger version of me sitting in front of Bangamata, her family surrounding her. The wristwatch that she had presented to me almost forty-five years ago was on the table in front of us. As soon as Mrs Sheikh Hasina spotted it, she pointed it out to Mr Modi, explaining what had been happening while the picture was taken. I was immediately called to take a picture along with the old photograph. Abha had shyly slipped back into the auditorium, but I pulled her to stand beside me as I stood with both the prime ministers. It was one of the most iconic pictures of my life with the prime ministers of Bangladesh and India on one side and Abha on the other.

This wasn't all. During the ceremony, when the prime minister of India addressed the people, in the middle of his speech, to my surprise, he narrated the story of the rescue that had been recounted to him a few minutes earlier. He ended his narrative by asking me to stand up so everybody could see me. He wanted people to be able to identify the face of the man he was speaking about. I stood up straight and looked around at everyone, before finally sitting down, my heart bursting with pride.

Towards the end of the ceremony, I was almost mobbed by the crowd, with people jostling to see me and talk to me about what they called a 'heroic act' all those years ago. It felt strange that in all these years I was just a non-entity and now, suddenly, within a few minutes I had been transformed into a celebrity.

We had deposited our phones with the authorities at the entrance and when we collected them, I was amazed to see the huge number of missed calls and messages from my friends and family. They had been watching the live relay of the event on television and had been calling to congratulate me and tell me how proud they were of me. I could barely keep up with answering all of them.

Laying my head on the pillow that night, I went over the events of the day and couldn't help but think how unique and special my life's journey had been. From being determined to rescue a family despite being unarmed so many years ago, to being reduced to near insignificance in the years that followed, to today . . . flanked by two prime ministers, while being the topic of their discussion. I smiled at the precious memory as I drifted off into a deeply contented slumber.

In the years after that, I have been invited to many events, where I have given talks, laid wreaths and taken part in discussions alongside many dignitaries, which were covered extensively by the media, television and print alike. The respect and honour that I continue to receive, even after so many years, is sometimes overwhelming.

They say that, when a soldier retires, he has to chart out a new course in life and discover new targets with the indomitable army spirit, so that he is not a parrot but an eagle. For a parrot talks too much and cannot fly high but the silent eagle has the willpower to touch the sky and soar above all storms. The hardest walk is the one you make alone . . . But that is the walk that makes you the strongest.

Acknowledgements

I remember the day this book was first discussed. I was still working on the last bits of my first book when, after work, I decided to visit my friend, Adheer, as his house was close to where I had gone for some research work. He, as usual, came down to my car to accompany me to his house and just as we were about to reach the little gate of Col Tara's house, my friend suddenly said, 'You should write a book on him.' He then went on to tell me how the colonel had singlehandedly rescued the prime minister of Bangladesh almost forty-nine years ago. I remember thinking to myself, 'How have I not even heard about this?' Which became my core motivation.

The rest, as they say, is history. So, my acknowledgements have to begin with thanking the man who actually sowed the seed of *The Lone Wolf*, my amazing and often crazy friend, Adheer Awasthi.

The actual process, however, began a few months later. By the time I got down to write the book proposal, after a few short interactions with Col Tara, we were well into the start of the unending lockdowns due to the pandemic. Needless to say, the days that followed were full of uncertainty and lots of restlessness. My first book was getting released during the pandemic, and here I was starting work on my second book. What I didn't realize at the time but do so now is that when most people around me were feeling lost and anxious, I managed to hold on to something that gave me reason to look forward to the next couple of months. The experience in itself was surreal and one that will always stay with me.

I have a few people to thank for it. My wonderful ex-editor Roshini Dadlani, for showing so much faith in me. I remember feeling excited and somewhat relaxed at the idea of being able to do this one with the same team. However, our association did not last for the entire duration due to some professional reasons. Nevertheless, I will always value the association we have.

Fortunately for me, Saloni Mital, from the team, continued being a part this time too and that helped a lot, so a big thanks to her.

Nicholas, my young and ever-smiling editor, became a part of this book towards the second half. Just in time for the second wave. I remember feeling anxious about having a new editor while half of the book was already done. However, just after our first call I was rest assured that the book was in good hands. Thank you for your invaluable inputs and support Nicholas, they helped me a lot.

While I was still trying to figure out the structure of the book and was constantly thinking of how to go about it, where to begin and where to end, I would have many conversations with my friends. The one person who made a big difference due to his insights and extended help with suggestions of the material that I could go through was my friend Moneet Sekhon, an army officer himself. He played a bigger role than perhaps he realizes himself.

I must thank one of my youngest and sweetest friends (actually my little sister's), Akshat Kumar, for many many reasons but mostly for always and always responding to all my calls and messages without so much as a frown, and there were MANY so it matters a lot.

Coming to the protagonist, the ever charming Col Ashok Tara and his wife Mrs Abha Tara. Thank you for sharing your story with me with an open heart, and always hosting me with immense warmth and affection. I will always be in awe of your heroic act and I hope to share that with all the readers through this book.

I want to thank Col Pankaj Gaur, for taking and addressing every single call and message that I made to him even when he didn't always have to.

I was most fortunate to be able to interact with Maj. Gen. Ian Cardozo who was a part of the war himself and who most graciously wrote the foreword for the book. There is so much to learn from him and I could not be more honoured that the foreword of *The Lone Wolf* came from him.

Lastly, this can never be complete without thanking Mrs Bhawna Dwivedi, my beautiful mother, for more things than I can mention here but in recent times, for always finding ways to talk about my books each time she meets people. It is beyond adorable. Diksha, my little sister, my partner in everything, my sounding board and my pole to lean on, for always standing by my side, no matter what.

I would end this with thanking my late father, Maj. C.B. Dwivedi, SM. He may not be around us physically, but there is no way any of the things I have done could ever be possible without his guiding light and watchful eye.

I know it. I believe it.

Notes

Chapter 4

1. 'Sheikh Mujib's 7 March Speech', Center for Bangladesh Genocide Research, http://www.cbgr1971.org/index.php/sheikh-mujib-s-march-7-speech-english-text.
2. Ibid.
3. Ibid.
4. Reuters, 'East Pakistani May Declare Secession', *New York Times*, 7 March 1971.
5. Sydney H. Schanberg, 'Sticks and Spears Against Tanks', *New York Times*, 29 March 1971.
6. Anthony Mascarenhas, 'Genocide', *Sunday Times*, 13 June 1971.
7. Ibid.

Chapter 6

1. Gary J. Bass, *The Blood Telegram: Nixon, Kissinger and a Forgotten Genocide* (Vintage, 2014).
2. Brig R.P. Singh, VSM (retired), 'How the Mukti Bahini Was Trained', *The Daily Star*, 24 May 2021.
3. Sydney H. Schanberg, 'Bengali Refugees in Squalor in India', *New York Times*, 22 May 1971.
4. Gary Tillery, *Working Class Mystic: A Spiritual Biography of George Harrison* (Quest Books, 2011), p. 100.

Chapter 8

1. Reuters, 'Mrs. Gandhi's Statement', *New York Times*, 4 December 1971.
2. Gary J. Bass, *The Blood Telegram: Nixon, Kissinger and a Forgotten Genocide* (Vintage, 2014).
3. Ibid.
4. UPI, 'Statements by Mrs. Gandhi on Truce and Surrender', *New York Times*, 17 December 1971.

Chapter 9

1. UPI, 'Statements by Mrs. Gandhi on Truce and Surrender', *New York Times*, 17 December 1971.
2. Charles Mohr, 'Dacca Captured', *New York Times*, 17 December 1971.
3. Ibid.
4. Sydney H. Schanberg, 'He Tells Full Story of Arrest and Detention', *New York Times*, 18 January 1972.
5. Anthony Lewis, 'Sheik Mujib, Free, Arrives in Britain', *New York Times*, 9 January 1972.